COMPETITIVE WINDSURFING

COMPETITIVE WINDSURFING

Penny Way and Rob Andrews

The Crowood Press

First published in 1990 by
The Crowood Press
Ramsbury, Marlborough,
Wiltshire SN8 2HE

British Library Cataloguing in Publication Data

Way, Penny
  Competitive Windsurfing.
  1. Wind surfing
  I. Title   II. Andrews, Rob
  797.3'3

  ISBN 1 85223 367 2

Acknowledgements

We would like to thank everybody who helped us in the production of this
book, in particular:

Paul Knights for taking the photographs.
Alison Claydon for her northern humour and invaluable assistance with the
photographs.
Mike Prout who provided the Fanatic boards and Art sails.
Ian Crowden and Joan Taylor of Shorebreak Designs who provided us with
harnesses and accessories.
Phil Nash of Select Fins.
Bournemouth Windsurfing Centre for letting us borrow anything else that
we needed!

All photographs are by Paul Knights except those listed below.
Bic: Figs 105 and 107.
Select: Figs 42 and 109.
Fanatic: Figs 75, 76, 80–82, 93–96, 100–103.
Rob Andrews: Figs 10, 111, 167, 187, 190.
David Eberlin: Figs 106 and 112.

Typeset by Consort Art Graphics, Exeter, Devon.
Printed in Great Britain by Butler & Tanner Ltd, Frome

Contents

Penny Way and Rob Andrews have probably more national and international competition experience than any other British couple. Penny's World Championship successes are legion while Rob introduces the solid backing of an international coach. This book pools their combined knowledge, and is without doubt the most comprehensive and detailed book I have read on the subject.

The reader is taken carefully and clearly through every step needed to become a world champion. Whether you started windsurfing yesterday or are a current champion, there is something useful for you in this book; even the competition organiser has not been left out.

This book will be your bible in an exciting and fast-growing sport.

Steven Schrier
Honorary Secretary, International Funboard Class Association and British Windsurfing Association

Penny Way is a highly successful competitor in international windsurfing. She has been the National Champion for eight years and has held other titles including the Women's World Championship in 1986. She is a qualified Royal Yachting Association (RYA) instructor and has coached worldwide.

Rob Andrews is an Olympic dinghy-sailing coach and also a qualified RYA windsurfing instructor. At the 1984 Olympics he instructed the British windsurfing team. Both of them contribute to the windsurfing and sailing press worldwide.

Eureka! Here is an informative up-to-date book on windsurfing competition. Newcomers should look no further since this provides an excellent background from which to start and progress.

There can be no more qualified authors than Penny and Rob who have been involved in racing at the highest level for a number of years. Penny has recently been campaigning for the Olympics and because of her impressive international record she is widely respected as far afield as China and North America.

I am sure you will learn from this book and I hope you enjoy your competitive windsurfing.

Ben Oakley
RYA National Competition Coach

I had clocked up less than fifteen hours of experience when a friend took me to a lake near Birmingham and told me I was about to enter my first race. I was filled with horror; 'I'm not good enough' I protested, but he insisted and so race I did. I found it enjoyable and invaluable in improving my windsurfing skills.

Having tasted the pleasures of racing at regional, national and international level I became involved in the organisation of windsurfing competition and now enjoy seeing windsurfers of all ages having fun racing.

It is good to see a book devoted to windsurfing competition especially by such highly qualified authors. See you at the next event!

Vicki Pashley
UKBSA secretary and event organiser

Introduction

There have been many books written about windsurfing but very few have concentrated on the competitive side of our sport. Windsurfing competitions are very popular at all levels, from those at the local club to the World Cup and Olympics. Competition has played a very important part in the development of windsurfing as a sport and in the equipment that is now used. The aim of this book is to encourage and help people to enter windsurfing competitions at all levels by explaining the disciplines and removing any mystery that may surround them.

Windsurfing was first brought into the eyes of the public in California in 1967 by an American computer analyst, Hoyle Schweitzer with his invention, the 'Windsurfer'. His enthusiasm and that of his family and friends was infectious and soon windsurfer class associations were forming all over the world. Each association ran its own weekend events consisting of competitive fun in the form of triangle racing, slalom, freestyle and marathon racing for everyone. Annually, the National Association members would meet up at the Windsurfer World Championships which became 'the event' in windsurfing. The windsurfer class association bred the stars of the 1980s – Robby Naish, Matt Schweitzer, Mike Waltze, Ken Winner and Rhonda Smith.

Windsurfing, like every other successful sport, is ideal for competition. Since the early days of the windsurfer class the sport has come a long way. The original competitive format of freestyle, slalom, course racing and marathon has been added to by the development of the short board which has brought a series of high wind events into the sport, such as wave sailing, speed and slalom.

Once you have learned to windsurf (which should take a week at the most if you have proper instruction), what do you do next? Recreational sailing soon becomes boring in light winds, and in stronger winds the battle of wanting better equipment and needing more money soon becomes painful! Competition is the answer. Unfortunately the word 'competition' sometimes scares potential windsurfers away, because immediately they feel that they are not good enough.

Competition should primarily be fun. There are competitions for every level of ability and furthermore it is the best way to improve your skills and become a better windsurfer. Many people have a preconceived idea that windsurfing competitions are for young males only. This is not the case as there are competitions and associations for both sexes and all ages of enthusiast, from a youth scheme run by the Royal Yachting Association, an organisation to encourage women to participate called Windsurfing Women UK , to the 'Seavets' who organise a series of events for the older windsurfer. Windsurfing is a sport for everybody from 5 to 95 years old. Contact addresses for the associations mentioned here can be found in Useful Addresses at the end of the book.

Any kind of competition encourages you to push your skills and equipment to the limits, to try and go faster, turn quicker and generally improve your board handling. You may not *win* your first events but you will *learn* a lot from them and it is this which will help to put you on the way to winning competitions. Even if you have no burning desire to win, competitions are an enjoyable form of entertainment and learning both on and off the water.

Introduction

In the following chapters we will describe each type of windsurfing competition from club racing to the World Cup and Olympics and explain how you can improve your technique, equipment, strategy, tactics and fitness so that you can be successful at these events. There are also some suggestions for you and your club so you can organise your own events and then easily persuade your fellow windsurfers to take part and have a good time. Competition is fun — so read on and soon you too will be able to enjoy it!

1 Your First Race

Just as the first time you stood on a windsurfer was a memorable occasion, so too is your first race. For just as that first sail introduced you to the sport of windsurfing, this first race will widen your horizons to all the competitive aspects of the sport. Racing allows you to learn so quickly that even if you decide later that you do not like competitions, your sailing will improve and you will derive so much more from the sport. Everyone should try to race at least once – it really does improve the gybing!

The race that we discuss in this chapter is similar to many races held at clubs or beaches all over the world. It is suitable for long boards, ideally over 3.7m with over 220l of volume (but if you are lighter than 11 stone then you can manage on a board with less volume). Such boards are the best for club racing in a variety of conditions.

Having decided that the best way to learn and meet other like-minded windsurfers is to race, your first task is to find out where the local races are held. Try contacting your local shop as they are often involved in the running of races in the area. However, you will need to organise a few items before you go racing for the first time and correct insurance cover should have the highest priority.

INSURANCE

You will need to decide whether you require third party or comprehensive cover; comprehensive insurance is the more expensive because it gives you better cover – if your equipment is damaged it will be replaced. If you just buy third party insurance you are only covered for damage to other people or their equipment.

Third party cover is the basic minimum that will be required when you start racing. In the UK a level of £500,000 worth of cover is the basic requirement, but check with your local windsurfing shop to see what the level is in the country you will be competing in. The shop will probably be able to sell you an insurance policy, but do take care to read the small print as there may be excess clauses for racing. This may mean that you will have to pay the first part of the claim and the insurance company will pay the balance.

SAIL NUMBERS

You will probably need to have a sail number on both sides of your sail for your first race. This sail number will be used to identify you on the water, both for safety and also for the results. In most countries you will be issued with a number that will be yours for life. Information about this can be obtained from your national authority. Again your local shop will be able to guide you in the right direction and supply you with the self-adhesive sail numbers that you will need. If you join the national authority you may receive your number as part of the service to members. The number for life is particularly helpful because you will not have to change the number from year to year.

Applying Sail Numbers

Sail numbers should only be applied to a sail when it is clean and dry. If in doubt wash the sail in fresh water and wait until it is thoroughly dry. Lay the sail out on a flat surface as shown in Fig 1. It is important to put the numbers on

Fig 1   Positioning the number on the sail with a small piece of the backing peeled off.

Fig 2   Peel off the backing slowly making sure that you press the number firmly on to the sail.

the starboard side first as these should always go above the numbers on the port side. The numbers on the starboard side should always be placed on the sail above the sail's half-height to aid identification. Simple numbers such as 1 can be appled directly to the sail, but more complicated figures such as 8 and 0 will need to be applied with the use of clear sticky-backed plastic. Place the clear plastic sticky side up on a flat surface and place the number face down on to the sticky side of the plastic. Remove the protective paper from the number and apply the whole sheet of plastic, with the number attached to the sail. Smooth over the plastic sheet and then remove it leaving the number attached to the sail. Once all the numbers are on your sail, smooth over them on a flat surface from the reverse side of the sail to increase adhesion.

If you need to remove old sail numbers you should take your sail to a sail maker or your local windsurfing shop as this process involves the use of solvents to get rid of the excess glue. If you do not remove this glue then dirt and sand will stick to the sail where the old numbers have been.

EQUIPMENT

Finally you will need a suitable board and rig for competition. You probably already have a board as most beginners' boards have enough volume to make ideal race boards at club level. The sail that came with your board is probably 6sq m which will be ideal in lighter winds, but you will need a smaller sail of approximately 4–5sq m for stronger winds. With these two sails you will be equipped for most weather.

Before you take part in your first race it is useful to go and watch the racing at your local club for a day and see what is involved. Have a chat with the local sailors – they will probably be very friendly and keen to have a new addition to their fleet. Try and find out as much information as possible about the racing so that you fully understand it. Ask if there is a booklet of race instructions that you can read.

YOUR FIRST RACE

Make sure that you are aware of the start time and when the sailors briefing will be and arrive in plenty of time. There is nothing worse than being hassled before the start – the important thing about this race is to have time to enjoy it.

Below is a checklist for your first race so that you know what to expect on the day.

1. Make sure that you have sufficient insurance cover for racing.
2. Put sail numbers on to your sails.
3. Find out the times of the races.
4. Arrive in plenty of time – allow at least one hour for rigging and changing.
5. Sign on at the clubhouse – there will possibly be a small entry fee.
Ask about signing off after races, or any other safety system that is used.
6. Check the local regulations.
7. Rig up and change.
8. Go to the briefing, make sure that you understand the course and the starting procedure.
9. Be on the water early – at least ten minutes before the start.
10. Make sure that you know where the marks are.
11. Be on the start line when the race starts. Good luck and enjoy it!

SAFETY

Check if you need to sign on before the start of the race – this consists of all competitors writing their name and sail number on a sheet of paper before they go on the water. When competitors return from the race they have to sign off to show that they have returned to the shore safely.

Another safety system used is the tally system. Each competitor is allocated a number that corresponds to a disc on the tally board. As you leave to go on to the water you take your disc with you and when you return to the shore you put your disc back. This system allows the race officer to see if anyone is missing, as, if your tally is not back on the board after the race has finished, you are assumed to be still at sea and the rescue craft will be sent to look for you.

Most clubs also insist that you wear a buoyancy aid. Most chest harnesses are buoyancy aids as well, but the lower seat harnesses do not have any useful buoyancy so you will have to wear a buoyancy aid with these.

There may be a small fee charged for racing which will be used to cover the cost of any rescue expenses and prizes for the winners of the series.

THE BRIEFING AND COURSE

Just before the first race of the day there will probably be a briefing where everybody meets up around the race officer and is told about the course and any alterations to the day's programme. Now is the time to ask questions if you are not sure about the course, starting procedure, etc.

GETTING OUT ON THE WATER

It is important to get out on the water at least ten minutes before the first timing signal – this

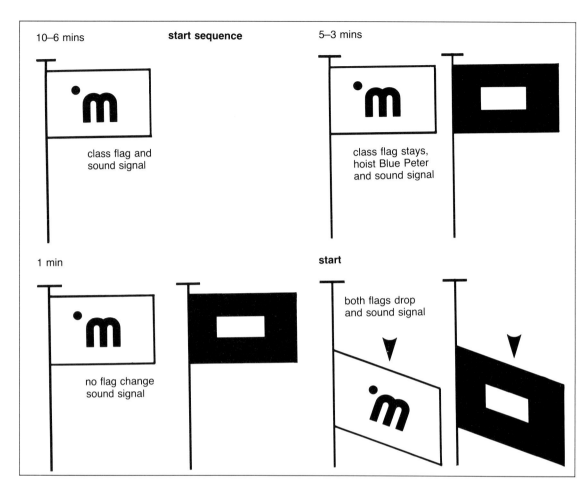

Fig 3 Start flag sequence.

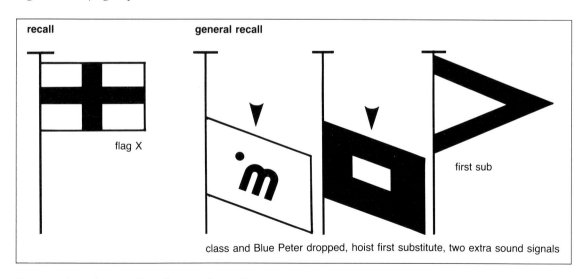

Fig 4 Flags for recall and general recall.

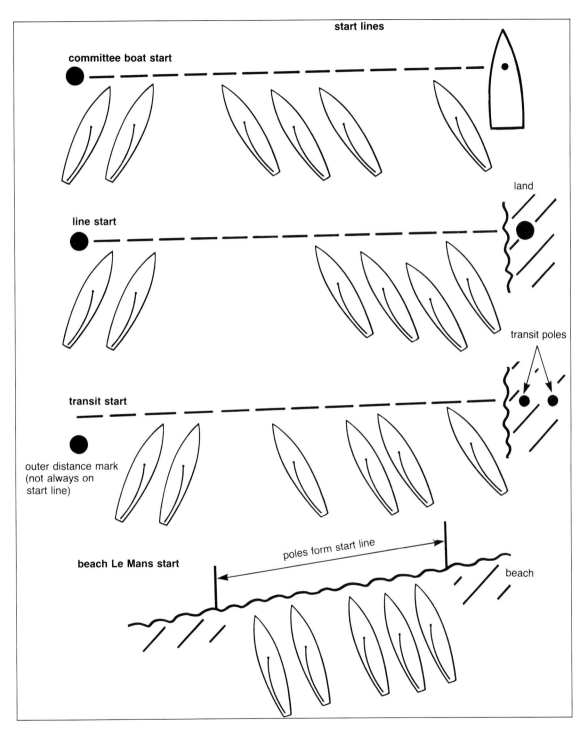

Fig 5 Examples of different start lines you may encounter.

will probably mean being prepared to go out as soon as the briefing has finished. This will give you the chance to relax on your board and get a feel for the conditions. Have a look at where the course is and make sure that you know which marks you are going to sail to. Sail to the start line and look towards the first mark, work out the route you are going to take to get there – it is better to calculate this now rather than when the start gun fires.

The briefing or the sailing instructions will have told you how the start line is marked – often in club races the start line will be on the shore. The start sequence will normally be signalled by flags and sound signals. The standard system is described here, but there are many different variations of this so read your sailing instructions carefully. The first signal is called the warning signal and will be followed by the preparatory signal – these will normally be three minutes apart, i.e. the warning signal will go six minutes before the start and the preparatory signal will go when there is only three minutes left before the start. (Note that some clubs use a ten minute and five minute system.) Most clubs also use a sound signal when there is only one minute left before the start. Shown previously in Fig 3 are the flags which will accompany these sound signals. It is a good idea to buy a flag chart which you can stick on your board and to use a waterproof digital watch to record the six or ten minute gun so that you know exactly how long you have before the starting gun.

By now the start time will be drawing near and you will be joined on the water by more boards. As the one minute sound signal approaches it is best to be on starboard tack (right hand closest to the mast), as you will then have right of way. Keep checking your watch and with just five seconds to go, power up your sail and accelerate away from the line. (Starting is studied in detail in Chapter 14.) On your way to the first mark remember that you have right of way on starboard and that if you are on port it is up to you to avoid anybody on a collision course with you. If the starting signal is followed immediately by another sound signal this means that some boards were over the line and, as shown in Fig 4 on page 12, flag X will be raised. If you knew you were over the line you must turn around, sail back and recross the line. If the start signal is followed by two sound signals and a blue and yellow flag is raised, this is a general recall and everyone must return to the start line to begin the start sequence again.

In Fig 5 you will see examples of different kinds of start lines that you may encounter at your local club. The first is a 'committee boat' start where you have to cross a line between a boat and a buoy, the second is a 'line' start between a buoy and a pole on the shore, the third is a 'transit' start where the start is between a buoy and two poles that line up with each other on the shore, and the fourth is a 'Le Mans' start where everybody starts from the beach.

The most important point about your first race is to enjoy it! In your next race try to improve on your previous position and try to work out where you made your mistakes. If you manage to eliminate these by good practice and preparation it will soon be others who will be looking at your sailing to work out where you get your extra speed from!

2 Funboard Racing

Funboard racing is the term used to describe a multi-discipline event sailed in 11kn of wind and above. The disciplines are: course racing which has developed from the original form of triangle racing; slalom racing; and wave performance. The wind limit means that all the equipment used is designed for strong winds and high speeds. A funboard event normally consists of either two or all three disciplines, with each discipline scoring equally to decide the final overall result. You will find that most national events will consist of only slalom and course racing because of the difficulty of finding a suitable venue to hold wave performance contests. For slalom and course racing the sea conditions do not matter so long as there is enough wind, but it is obviously not possible to hold a wave contest without any waves!

Competitive funboard racing is run internationally by two organisations – the International Funboard Class Association (IFCA) who organise racing for production funboards and the Professional Boardsailors' Association (PBA), who organise racing for custom boards. The IFCA organise annually the Production Board World Championships which consists of course racing and slalom. This championship is well supported by the manufacturers as the boards that are raced have to be identical to those that can be bought in shops. The official definition of a production funboard is 'one being built in a mould in a minimum series of 500 identical hulls'.

The PBA organise a series of events making up the World Cup, which consist of course racing, slalom and wave performance. The competitors may use custom boards to try and gain an edge over their rivals. These boards tend to be the prototypes for the eventual production boards and most major manufacturers have a team of competitors competing in the World Cup which takes them to all corners of the world with events as far afield as Japan, France, Hawaii, Spain, Portugal and Australia.

In the following chapters you will find an explanation of the funboard disciplines, with a section on the techniques needed and some useful practice exercises. In a sport such as windsurfing it is very easy just to blast up and down and have a good time instead of practising specific points which you find difficult. Practising isn't always as much fun, but it is a better way to improve!

3 Course Racing

Course racing is the discipline most often raced at funboard events because it is not so dependent on perfect conditions. As mentioned previously, course racing is similar to Olympic triangle racing, but, as you can see in Fig 6, the course has been designed for higher winds with longer and tighter reaches, more gybes and no run, which allows for exciting action for both competitors and spectators.

The standard course used in funboard racing is shown in Fig 6. The modified course that can be used if the conditions are very rough and the standard course cannot be set is shown over the page in Fig 7.

COURSE DESCRIPTION AND RACING STRATEGY

The course race can be broken up into four stages – the start, the upwind leg, the reaches and the gybes.

The Start

The start line will be placed 1,000–1,500m directly downwind of the first mark. Once the start flag has been raised competitors have to pass through this line towards the first mark. For starting tactics see Chapter 14. Basically the aim is to start as quickly as possible at the favoured end of the line in clear air.

The Upwind Leg

This can be between 1,000–1,500m long, but due to the fact that you cannot sail straight into the wind, you will have to sail considerably further than this. If you have had a good start

the upwind leg is a lot easier to sail because you should not be affected by the 'dirty wind' of other sails. If you have had a bad start, try and get clear of other boards and just aim to get up a good speed. When you are sailing upwind to the first mark it is important not to tack too often as you will lose speed and increase the possibility of making mistakes. It is quite hard to tack high wind course racing boards because of their low volume and large sails. Only tack when you have a good reason – such as the need to tack again to get to the mark, or when you are positive that you have been headed – *see* Chapter 14. If you are on port and heading for someone who has the right of way on starboard tack, it is often best to go behind them rather than lose speed by tacking. Try always to approach the windward mark on starboard so that you are not caught having to tack on top of the buoy, surrounded by a group of other racers.

The Reaching Legs

The standard funboard course consists of a minimum of 3,400m and a maximum of 7,000m of reaching – reaching speed is crucial in course racing. The course is sailed twice and the finish line is at the end of the reaching legs and is to leeward of the committee boat. The reaching finish gives even more importance to good reaching speed. If you need to overtake someone on a reach try always to go to windward of them so that you get clean air. However make sure that you are not taken too far upwind; if this starts to happen, quickly alter course and duck underneath the board you are overtaking.

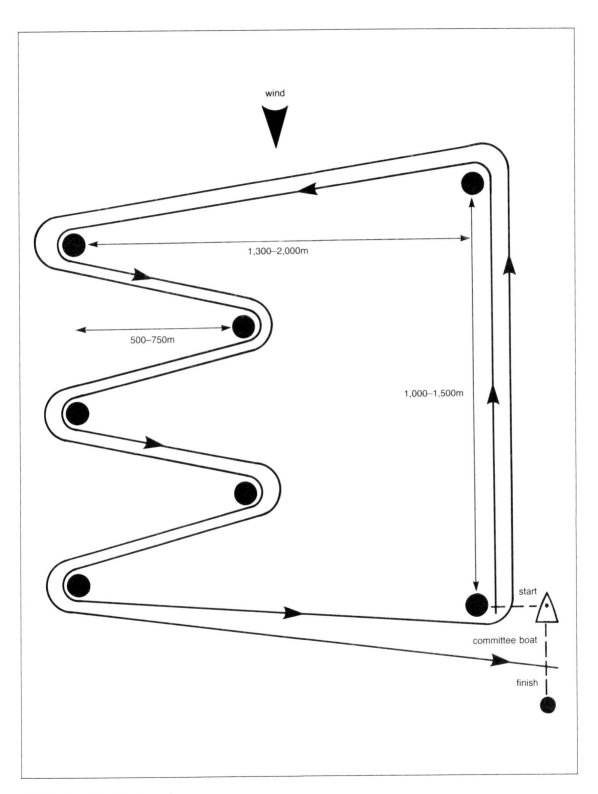

wind

1,300–2,000m

500–750m

1,000–1,500m

start

committee boat

finish

Fig 6   Standard funboard course.

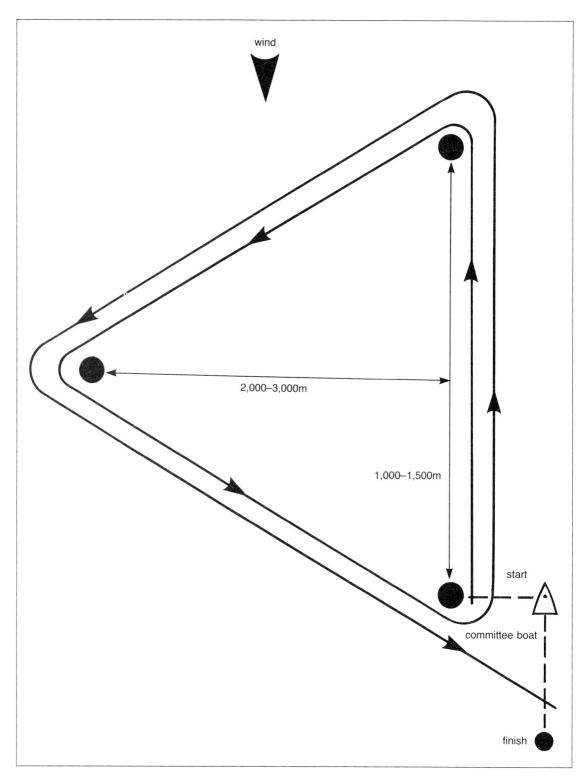

Fig 7   Modified course to be used in very rough conditions.

Gybing

The standard course consists of ten gybes. The long course racing board is not easy to gybe and the technique for this manoeuvre will be found in the course racing technique section later in this chapter. When approaching marks try to always have the inside position so that you have right of way around the marks and are in a good position for the next leg of the course – *see* Chapter 13.

STARTING SIGNALS

Starting signals are made from the committee boat on the start line. Unless otherwise prescribed by the sailing instructions which you will be given when you enter for the event, the starting signals will be as below.

Six minutes before start – sound signal and RED flag displayed.
Three minutes before start – sound signal and YELLOW flag displayed.
At start – sound signal and GREEN flag displayed.

Normally there will also be a sound signal one minute before the start. It is important to remember that the flags are more important than the sound signals – if you have not heard the gun but the flag has gone up, the flag counts. Make sure that you read the sailing instructions carefully and consult the relevant rule books if there is something that you do not understand. There is nothing worse than losing places or even a race because you didn't have time to read the sailing instructions.

SCORING

POSITION	POINTS
1st	0.7
2nd	2
3rd	3
4th	4, etc

Only one course race has to be held for the event to be counted. If more than three races are held, competitors are then allowed to discard their worst race. Below is a chart showing the number of discards that are allowed for the number of races held.

NUMBER OF RACES	NUMBER OF DISCARDS
1–3	0
4–6	1
7–10	2
11 or more	3

The rules of windsurfing are discussed in Chapter 13, where you will find the rules for course racing.

COURSE RACING EQUIPMENT

Boards

For events organised by the IFCA the boards raced have to be series production boards. The board shown over the page in Fig 8 is a Fanatic Cat, one of the most successful production boards, having won the 1987 Production World Championships. Its technical details are:

Nose – double concave on V basis.
Mid section – double concave.
Tail – flat V.
Rails – full rails with tucked-under edge becoming sharper and flatter towards tail.

*Fig 8 The Fanatic Ultra Cat used
for course racing.*

Length – 374cm.
Width – 65cm.
Weight – 13.2kg.
Volume – 210l.

The custom course racing boards used at PBA events all look very similar to production boards, but they are specially built to minimise weight which makes them both more expensive and more fragile than production boards. Prototype boards are tried and tested at World Cup events and the successful designs are then put into production.

In very strong winds racers often use their slalom boards for course racing as the funboard courses are so reaching-orientated that it pays to use a smaller, fast reaching board rather than struggle around the course on a larger board.

You have to be good at sailing your slalom board upwind to try this! Slalom boards used for course racing are fitted with large skegs to improve their upwind performance and the sail size is one size down from that which would be used on a course racing board.

Course Racing Rigs

The sails used for course racing are all camber-induced and are therefore very powerful and stable. Most competitors have a quiver of seven or eight sails ranging from 4 to 8sq m, and use the same sails for both slalom and course racing. The smallest sail normally used in course racing is 5sq m, but this may vary in extreme conditions. Booms and masts used are

*Fig 9 A 7.5 Art camber-induced
sail.*

very stiff and light and usually made of aluminium or carbon fibre. Most racers have at least five different sized rigs ready to sail on the beach which means having a plentiful supply of masts, booms, UJs, harness lines, etc. The sail that is finally chosen for the race conditions, should be the biggest that can be handled upwind in the conditions – it is important to have a large sail so that the board is not underpowered downwind. It is very important to have adequate downhaul tension on these sails as this controls the fullness of the sail, as the windier it is the more downhaul you will need. However, if you apply too much downhaul, you may cause the sail to distort.

Boom Height

Most competitors sail with the boom at shoulder height for course racing.

Harnesses and Lines

For course racing the low seat harness with long harness lines is the most popular. Some competitors use adjustable harness lines so that they can be shortened when they are overpowered going upwind and lengthened for the downwind legs. Low seat harnesses are now preferred for course racing, slalom and speed sailing. The seat harness is more efficient because the hook is positioned lower on the body, which means that the load is taken from a lower centre of gravity so that it can take more force and bigger sails can be used. Unlike chest and waist harnesses, the seat harness is very firmly attached to the body with leg straps and does not ride up when pulled by a strong gust. The seat harness is also much better for the back as the force is mostly taken by the legs – the lower back is well protected. Because the

Fig 10   A seat harness.

hook position of the seat harness is much lower than with other harnesses it is important to use longer lines. The lines need to be just long enough for you to sail with straight arms.

At World Cup events the racers wear weight jackets to help them handle a bigger sail in both course racing and slalom. Weight jackets are made of lead or water bottles and weigh between 4 and 6kg. The IFCA have banned the use of weight jackets from their events – if you are thinking of trying one out on other occasions make sure you are fit enough to wear it and have sufficient buoyancy to keep you afloat!

Course Racing Skegs

Course racing skegs are the biggest used in any discipline because of the large size of the board. It is very important to have a large, stiff and

Fig 11   A weight jacket.

Fig 12   The weight jacket is filled with water bottles weighing 2kg each.

Fig 13   A course racing skeg.

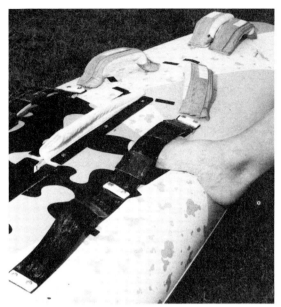

Fig 14   Lightweight plastic footstraps.

well-fitting skeg – if not you will find that the board is uncontrollable on the reaches and tends to slide sideways and spin out. A large skeg also helps the board to sail upwind. The important qualities of a good skeg are that it should be stiff, light and a good shape, mostly made out of carbon fibre or foam. Because of the pressure on skegs at high speed, the new skeg boxes have to be very strong and some are actually tied through the deck of the board. If you are still spinning out with a good skeg try moving it further forwards in the skeg box.

Footstraps

Footstrap positions on a course racing board are a very personal decision (*see* Fig 14). On the reaches you want to be able to stand as far

back on the board as possible without having to move forwards of the straps to gybe. If you have shorter legs you will need your reaching straps to be closer together than someone with longer legs needs. For the upwind stages you will want two beating straps quite far back on either side of the board with the back strap very close to your front reaching strap. Do not put these straps too far out on the rail of the board or they will be dragging in the water. Make sure that the beating straps are the correct size, as unlike reaching straps you want only your toes to be under them – if they are too big your whole foot will slide underneath and you will not be able to rail the board. Once you have worked out your strap positions, use only one set – there is more to trip over with lots of straps on the board, and they also add to its weight when wet. Some racers replace their padded straps with nylon webbing which is lightweight and does not soak up water.

Fig 15   *This photograph shows the long beating straps and a single set of reaching straps.*

COURSE RACING TECHNIQUES AND EXERCISES

The following techniques are necessary for success in course racing. In each case the technique is described and then practice exercises are suggested which can be used to perfect the technique. The best way to perfect a skill is by repetition, but if you keep falling in the water and are not able to grasp the skill, it is best to leave the exercise and come back to it later with a fresh mind – it is more than likely that you will be able to do it perfectly the next time! Try to do each exercise ten times and then leave it, come back to it after a short time and try and do it three times perfectly. Once you have mastered an exercise, try to do it with your eyes closed and you will find that you develop a feel for the forces acting on your board and sail and become much more aware of the movements that you are making. This is best done in a group of people with someone on the look-out in case an ocean liner comes your way!

Starting

The tactics of starting are discussed more fully in Chapter 14. The most important starting technique when starting among a large fleet is board control. You need to be able to jostle for position and exit from situations with a great degree of confidence if you are to get a good start.

The following exercise is easy to carry out and can be done on your own. You need one marker buoy which you can hit without destroying it or your board! This exercise will help you to control your position on the line.

Fig 16   *Practising start line board control next to a mark.*

1. Approach the buoy from downwind and bring the nose of your board as close to it as possible without actually touching it, as shown in Fig 16.
2. Try to remain in this position using your sail to hold you there. If you need to back off a bit, back the sail slightly. If you are drifting downwind, sheet in and get back into position.
3. Try to hold this position for one minute. As you improve, increase the time.

Mast Tracks and Centreboards

Most course racing boards are now sold with mast tracks designed to move the position of your mast foot as you sail on different points of the wind. The mast tracks on wave, slalom and speed boards are not normally designed to be adjusted while sailing. It is very important to learn to adjust your mast foot position on your course racing board, for as well as improving your speed, it will make the board much easier to sail.

When to Move Your Mast Foot

To make this easier to explain, imagine the mast track divided into thirds – the front third, middle and back. When you are sailing upwind, i.e. from the start line, you should have your mast foot in the front section of the track. When you are sailing on a reach in over 11kn of wind you should have the mast foot in the rear section of the track.

The exceptions to this are:

1. When you are sailing upwind you should have the mast foot as far forward as possible, but if the nose starts to go under, bring it back a little.
2. If you are sailing in minimal wind conditions and have difficulty railing the board, try putting the mast foot nearer the centre of the mast track – this will encourage the board to rail.
3. On reaching legs if the wind is light or the reach very broad, you will find that the tail of the board will begin to drag with the mast foot

Figs 17–19 Moving the mast forwards.

Fig 18

Fig 19

in the back of the track. To avoid this, move the mast foot nearer to the centre of the track.

How to Move Your Mast Foot

Most mast tracks have a pedal at the back of the track that you depress for the mast foot to slide forwards or back along the track until you remove your foot, when the mast foot will lock into position.

To Move Your Mast Foot Forwards

It is easiest to do this when you are sailing upwind. Press down on the track pedal with your front foot, push down and forwards through the boom and the mast foot will slide forwards. If the track is stiff, use the knee of your front leg to help push the mast forwards.

To Move Your Mast Foot Backwards

It is easiest to do this when you are sailing on a close reach. Press down on the track pedal with your front foot, push down on the boom and pull it towards you to pull the mast foot back. If the track is stiff, try putting your front hand on the mast just down from the boom connection to help you pull the mast back along the track.

Using a Retracting Centreboard

All course racing boards now have fully retracting centreboards. As a general rule whenever you are sailing upwind your centreboard should be fully down and whenever you are sailing downwind your centreboard should be fully retracted, but there are some exceptions to this rule (two of which are given over the page).

Figs 20–2   Moving the mast foot back.

Fig 21

Fig 22

1. If you become overpowered when sailing upwind in a strong breeze you will find that by knocking your centreboard back slightly you can stop the board from railing up and this will improve your handling of the conditions. Be careful that you do not slide too far off the wind. To correct this apply more pressure with your back leg to keep the board heading up into the wind.

2. When the wind is light and you are sailing on a reach and not able to plane, you can often improve the performance of your board by leaving the centreboard down and sailing the board on its rail (*see* the following section for information on railing).

Practice Exercise For Moving Your Mast Track and Centreboard

Set up a small course using three buoys positioned so that you have an upwind leg and two long reaches. Mark No 1 is the leeward mark, No 2 the windward mark and No 3 the reaching mark.

1. Start at mark No 1 and position the mast track and centreboard in their upwind positions – mast track forwards and centreboard down.

2. Sail upwind to mark No 2. Retract your centreboard and bear away around the mark. Once you are on the reach, pull your mast track back.

3. Gybe around mark No 3 and reach back to mark No 1 – keep your centreboard retracted and mast track back.

4. Carve the board around mark No 1 trying to get as close to it as possible. Once you are pointing on your upwind course, put the centreboard down and slide the mast track forwards.

5. Practice covering this course as quickly as possible, always making sure you move your mast track and centreboard as quickly and smoothly as possible. If you are finding the course too easy, move the marks closer together and if you are finding it hard, move the marks further apart.

Upwind Sailing on Course Racing Boards

Sailing upwind on a course racing board is a skill which can make a lot of difference to your performance in a race. If you get upwind to the first mark in a good position, you are well set up for the rest of the race. Sailing fast upwind on a course board is all about getting everything right for the conditions – mast track positions, centreboard position, the amount that you rail the board and the angle to the wind and waves that you choose to sail at. Selecting your mast foot and centreboard positions have been covered in the previous sections; here we will concentrate on railing technique and sailing angle.

Railing

Railing is a technique used to improve a board's upwind performance. The windward rail is allowed to lift slightly but not so much that the footstraps on the leeward rail catch in the water. This is a very subtle technique achieved by putting most of the body-weight on the rig and toes instead of the windward rail (*see* Fig 23 on page 30). Try to keep the rig upright so that you can use its full power. If you are trying to get the board to rail in very light winds you will find it easier if you pull the mast foot back slightly and push on the daggerboard top to encourage the board to rail.

This is a technique that works well in light to moderate winds, but in strong winds you will find that the problem is in stopping the windward rail from lifting. The way to achieve this is to have the mast track well forwards and to rake the centreboard back slightly.

Upwind in Strong Winds

In stronger winds you should be using the beating straps, which should be positioned near the reaching straps so that you can get well back on the board (*see* the section on footstraps

Fig 23   Railing a course racing board upwind.

Fig 24   Sailing upwind using the beating foot straps.

on page 23). The straps will help to keep your feet in a set position, which is much faster than having your weight moving around the board, and will prevent your feet from being wiped off the board by a monster wave. You should try to lean forwards from the straps; you will find that all of the pressure is taken by your back leg. If you start to become overpowered, try to pull the rig more over on top of you.

Your Sailing Angle

It is important to sail at exactly the right angle to the wind, but unfortunately this is only possible to judge after hours of practice. If you sail too close to the wind the board will stall and if you sail too far away you will have to cover a greater distance to get to the mark. You need to find a good balance when you are going at maximum speed as close to the wind as possible.

Practice Exercise for Upwind Sailing

The best way to practise your upwind sailing is to work together with a partner.

1. To do this exercise successfully, you need two people with similar equipment and board speed.
2. Decide who is to be the control board – this person does not change their equipment –

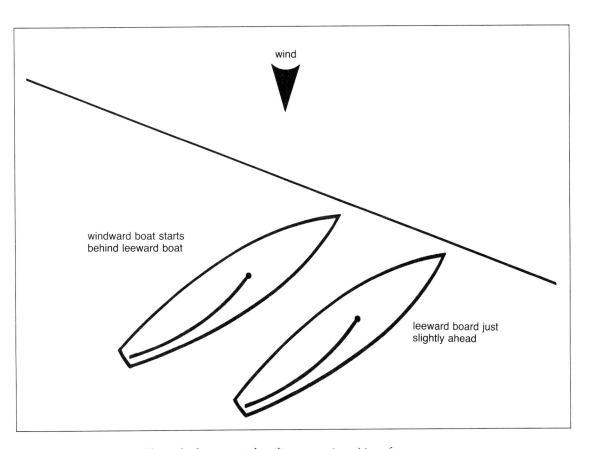

wind

windward boat starts
behind leeward boat

leeward board just
slightly ahead

*Fig 25   Positioning of boards for upwind sailing exercise. Aim: for
neither board to have an advantage at the start.*

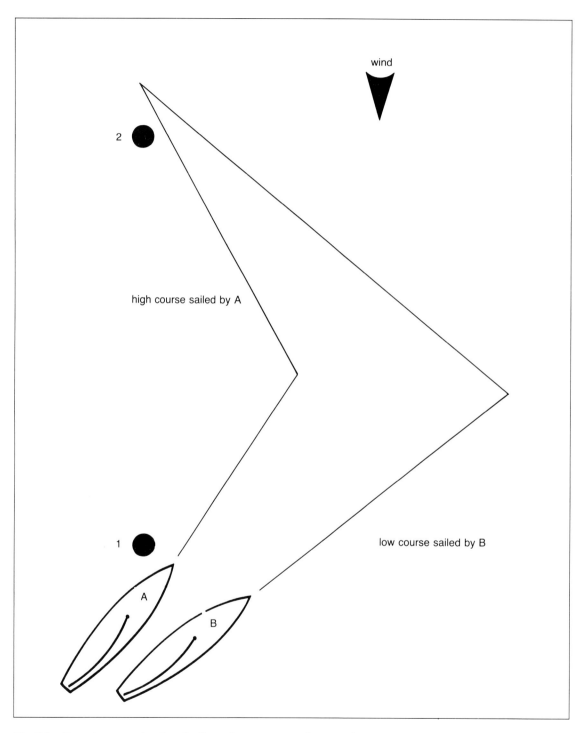

Fig 26   Practice exercise for finding the correct sailing angle.

and who is to be the tester – the person who tries different stances and tuning positions.

3. Set up your equipment identically – mast, foot positions, etc. and start sailing upwind together, with the leeward board just slightly ahead so that you are equally placed – *see* Fig 25 on page 31. Make sure that the leeward board is far enough downwind not to disrupt the wind of the windward board.

4. As soon as you have established a similar board speed, the tester should try altering one item at a time, for example the centreboard rake, while the sailor of the control board does not alter any equipment. By this method you should be able to reach some positive conclusions.

5. Record your results in your training diary (*see* Chapter 12).

Practice Exercise for
Finding the Correct Sailing Angle

You will also need a partner for this exercise. Choose two buoys that are directly in line with the wind. The aim is to sail from the downwind mark to the upwind mark starting at the same time and sailing on the same side of the beat. One of you will decide to sail low and the other high. The board that is going to sail low will start to leeward of the board that is going to sail the high course (*see* Fig 26).

1. Make sure that your equipment is set up identically and that you have similar board speeds. Start at the bottom mark as you did with the previous exercise, with the leeward board starting fractionally ahead of the windward.

2. Sail on this tack until you are both on your lay line for the windward mark and then tack.

3. When you get to the windward mark, sail back to mark No 1 and change over to do the exercise again.

You will be able to draw your own conclusions as to the best angle to sail at with your equipment in the conditions. You will probably find in rough and windy conditions that it is best to sail a lower course than in flat water and light conditions.

Tacking

Because of the lack of volume in the nose of course racing boards and the camber-induced sails that are used with them, tacking can sometimes cause a few problems. In a course race you will have to tack an average of fifteen times, so it is important to have a good technique.

1. As you approach the tack, start luffing the board by pushing the back of the board away from you with your back foot, remove your feet from the straps and pull in with your back hand (*see* Fig 27).

2. Continue pulling in with your back hand, move your feet forwards, keeping pressure on the back foot to help the board to turn (*see* Fig 28).

3. As the board comes round into the wind, move your back hand to the front of the boom and transfer your weight to your front foot, sail the board past the eye of the wind and let go with your old front hand. Quickly move around the mast and at the same time throw the mast forwards with your old back hand (*see* Fig 29).

4. Sheet in with what has now become your back hand (Fig 30). As you regain speed move both hands on to the boom (Fig 31) and get into the straps again (*see* Fig 32).

The most important points are to move around the mast quickly and to throw the rig forward as you go around.

Practice Exercise for Tacking

This is an exercise that you can easily do by yourself. Start in a position from where you can sail upwind. Set your watch to sound an alarm in five minutes. Sail upwind counting every second and when you reach ten – tack – concentrating on the correct technique. As soon as you start sailing on the new tack start counting again and tack every ten seconds until

Figs 27–32 Tacking a course racing board.

Fig 28

Fig 29

Fig 30

Fig 31

Fig 32

the five minutes has elapsed. If you find this exercise difficult, increase the interval between tacks to twenty seconds.

Tacking is much harder in rough seas and strong winds. Once you have mastered the art in flat water and light winds, it is time to progress to the sea. When you are trying to tack in waves, pick the correct moment so that you are not about to tack just as a large wave is approaching! Being able to tack out of the way of another competitor without losing speed is a very useful skill to acquire.

The Reaching Stance for Course Racing Boards

As mentioned earlier the reaching legs in a funboard course can be up to 7,000m, so good reaching speed is vital.

Once you have rounded the windward mark, retract your centreboard, pull your mast foot to the back of the track, put your feet into the reaching straps and hook in to your harness. Try to always use the straps that are furthest back, but if the wind is light you may have to stand further forward. Once you are in the straps you will find that you have to lean forwards to prevent the board from heading into the wind. Your arms should be at full stretch with your legs locked out and toes pointed. Once you are planing, sail the board as flat as possible, keeping the rig upright so that you can use its full power. If you begin to get overpowered, pull the sail over on top of you slightly and bear away instead of sheeting out. Pull in and down with your back hand so that you bring the bottom of the sail down to the level of the board. This brings the centre of effort down and back and enables you to stand back on the tail to reduce wetted surface and move the centre of lateral resistance back. Do not bring the sail down so far that the battens drag in the water. If you have problems spinning out it is probably because you are not leaning far enough forwards or maybe you do not have a very good skeg on your board (*see* section on skegs, page 22–3).

Practice Exercise for Reaching on a Course or Slalom Board

The problem that you may find with trying to reach in planing conditions on course racing or slalom boards is that you are unable to get your feet in the back footstraps without the board trying to head up into wind and stop! This happens because you are putting all your weight on the back of the board and pivoting the front of the board into the wind. The solution is to lean forwards on the boom to put more pressure through the mast foot – this will keep the nose of the board away from the wind. This stance feels very awkward to start with but is very comfortable once you get used to it. A good way of practising this stance when there is not enough wind to get into the footstraps is to retract the centreboard, put your mast track in the middle position, sail on a reach and then try to drop your front leg into the water up to your thigh by bending your back leg. You will then automatically be putting all your weight through the mast and the mastfoot to stop the board from heading up into the wind. Once you have done this successfully in one direction, tack, and try it the other way. It is important when learning any new manoeuvre to be able to do it on both tacks. So now, when you try getting into your footstraps in a stronger wind, you will know what it feels like to put pressure through the mast foot.

To practise reaching quickly it is best to try it with a partner. When you sail against someone of a similar standard you will tend to push yourself much harder than you would if you were sailing alone. Concentrate on your stance as explained above and think all the time about pushing yourself to go faster.

Carve Gybing on a Course Racing Board

This manoeuvre is generally harder on a course racing board than on a smaller board because

Fig 33   The reaching stance on a course racing board.

Fig 34   Sailing with one leg in the water to practise the reaching stance.

of its larger area. You have more board to control in the water. You have to have speed to practise this gybe.

1. Sail on to a broad reach, unhook from your harness but stay in the footstraps and keep up your speed (*see* Fig 35).
2. Take your back foot out of the strap and place it further forward on the leeward rail, bending your knees slightly (Fig 36). To start the turn push down on your leeward rail with your back foot and lift up the windward rail with your front foot which is still in the strap. Continue to bend your knees, which should be pointing in towards the centre of the turn (*see* Fig 37).
3. Do not try to turn the board too tightly or you will lose speed. Keep your arms relatively straight throughout the turn to keep the rig upright and maintain full power throughout (*see* Fig 38).
4. Slowly let out with your back hand throughout the turn, as the board turns through 180 degrees, sail clew first for a second, then let go with your back hand (Fig 39). As the sail flips, take hold of the mast with your new front hand and quickly change your feet around – taking care not to stand too far back or the board will spin into the wind (*see* Fig 40).
5. Sheet in with your new back hand, pump to gain speed and put your feet back into the straps.

Practice Exercises for
Gybing in Slalom and Course Races

When you are practising these gybes it is very important to put in 100 per cent effort. The

Figs 35–40   Carve gybing a course racing board.

Fig 36

Fig 37

Fig 38

Fig 39

Fig 40

only way that you will make your board gybe more smoothly and quickly is by falling off a lot in practice. It is not perhaps the most pleasant of things to be doing on a cold wet day, but it will certainly pay off when it comes to the racing season! You will need two buoys set across the wind so that you can sail a figure-of-eight course reaching between them (*see* Fig 41).

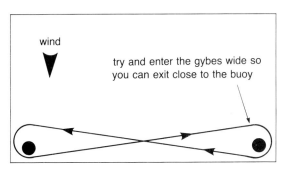

Fig 41   Gybing exercise.

This exercise is best performed with a group of sailors so that you can simulate high speed jostling at marks. Decide how many times you are going to sail the course and then start in a group. On the reaches, concentrate on getting as much speed out of your equipment as possible. At the gybes try to get around as quickly and as close to the mark as possible. Your aim is to come out of the turn almost touching the mark. Once out of the turn, practise pumping the board on to the next wave to increase your speed. You should be coming out of the turn at the same speed that you went in at!

This is also a good exercise to practise on your own. Remember to push yourself hard. Set yourself a goal to sail the course perfectly perhaps ten times before going on to another exercise.

4 Slalom Racing

Slalom racing is a very spectator-orientated form of funboard racing. It is easy to watch, exciting and provides good, fast racing. Competitors start together in heats of eight from the beach, or a line start at sea. They then proceed around a course consisting of between two and six buoys which are never far from the shore. The finish is either between two flags on the beach, or at sea between a flag and the race boat. The first four from each heat usually go through to the next round.

THE ELIMINATION PROCESS

Fig 42 shows a typical elimination ladder with the names of the competitors distributed evenly by lot on the ladder. Each group lot sail against each other in heats – the winners going through as shown.

THE SLALOM COURSE

Fig 43 shows the standard slalom course, while Fig 44 is used only when it is impossible to set the course in Fig 43.
Note that for the two buoy slalom course, the start can be from the beach or the water. With an onshore wind the start should usually be from the water.

As you can see from the course diagrams, there is no upwind sailing in slalom racing, unlike in course racing. The course consists of long reaching legs so that the emphasis is on each individual sailor achieving good reaching speed and gybing technique. *See* page 45 for ways to improve these skills.

SLALOM STRATEGY

Slalom racing is about flat out board speed and gybing through 90 degrees – two contradicting elements which are both studied later in this chapter.

Once you have mastered these skills however, you still have to have a sound race strategy to win at slalom racing. The slalom race can be split into three sections – the start, the reaches and the gybes.

The Start

In some slalom races a good start is 95 per cent of the race – once you have got ahead you will have clear wind and water and should be able to move off from the pack. The start sequence for slalom is the same as that for course racing and most slalom starts are on the water rather than from the beach. It is imperative to cross the start line at maximum speed, so you have to do dummy runs using transits to work out how long it takes to get from a spot you can easily find to the start line. It is important to have a watch that you can see and set easily. In many slalom races the organisers use instant photo equipment to see who may have been over the line at the start – if you are over the line and do not return you are disqualified. Most slalom start lines are very short, so it is more important to get a good, clean, fast start rather than get to the favoured end.

The Reaches

Once you are clear of the start it is important to concentrate on your speed and not allow people to overtake you. If you are ahead, try to sail the

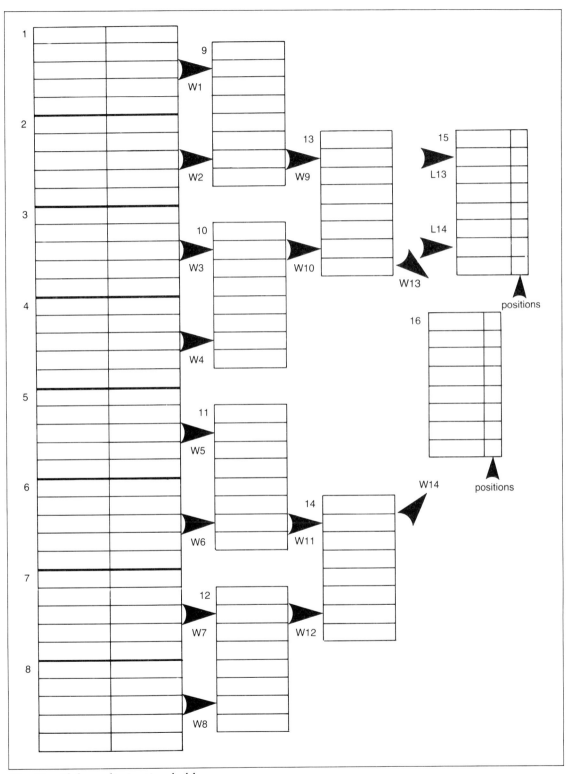

Fig 42   Slalom elimination ladder.

43

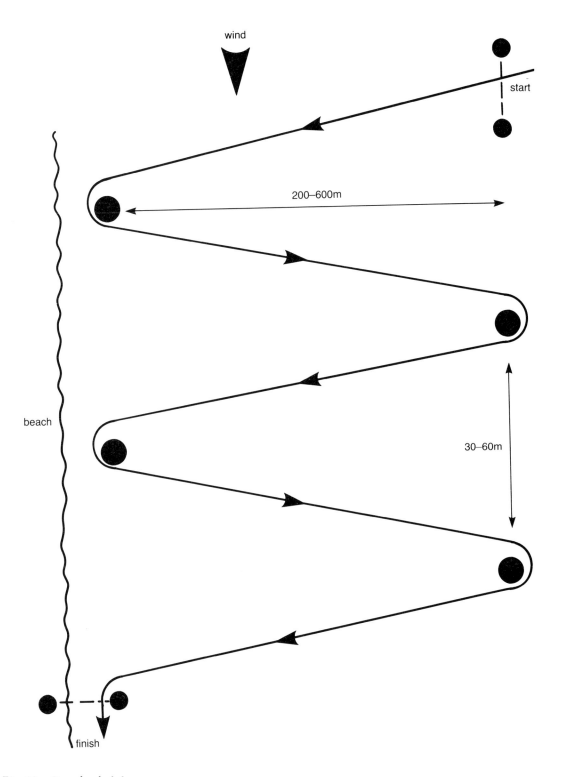

Fig 43   Standard slalom course.

44

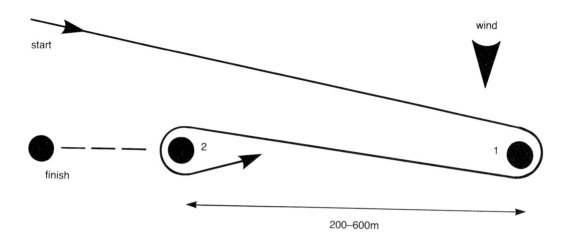

(course is 3–5 times around mark 1)

Fig 44   Two buoy slalom course.

most direct line to the first mark. If people try to overtake you to windward, go upwind with them and they should not be able to get through. If they try to get through to leeward, bear away so that they are unable to do so. Always remember that you are racing against seven other people, not just one. If you need to overtake the person in front of you, try to do it to windward – if they try to take you upwind, try to make a quick alteration of course to take you underneath them when they are not expecting it.

The Gybes

As you approach the gybe mark, think where you want to be on your exit. If you are in the lead you have an easy task, come into the mark high so that you can exit from it as close as possible. If you are not first there are likely to be other sailors around the mark, so do not try to cut inside, unless you are certain of your rules and ability – high speed crashes can be dangerous and expensive. Try to do the fastest

gybe you can to bring you out of the mark as high as possible for the next leg without hitting any of the obstacles in the water!

Success in slalom racing is all about practice! When you go out on the water you must be prepared to fall into the water time after time to practise your high speed gybes!

RULES

As we have already mentioned, it is important to be aware of the rules before competing and these are found in Chapter 13 of this book. For more details consult the funboard section of the IYRU racing rules.

STARTING AND FINISHING PROCEDURE

The starting system is the same as for course racing with a red, orange and green flag at three-minute intervals. The funboard rules state that the starting line can be:

1. A rope which is lying on the beach near the water and which has been stretched taut between two stakes. The rope shall have numbered stations spaced 5m apart along its length, and equal in number to the maximum number of starters.
2. A line between two marks.
3. Any other line specified in the sailing instructions.

The finishing line shall be:

1. A line between a mark and a stationary post on the beach. The post shall be marked by a blue flag, prominently displayed.
2. A line between two marks.
3. Any other line as specified in the sailing instructions.

SCORING

The chart below shows the scoring system for slalom. At least one elimination series has to be proceeded until the field has been reduced to the last eight competitors for the discipline to count as part of the event.

When more than two slalom eliminations have been held the competitors are allowed to discard their worst race. The table below shows the discard system that is used.

NUMBER OF RACES	NUMBER OF DISCARDS
1–2	0
3–4	1
5–7	2
8 or more	3

SLALOM EQUIPMENT

A slalom board is normally between 260 and 290cm long, depending on the wind strength and weight of the person they are designed for. Slalom competitions take place in winds from 11kn upwards, so competitors often need two boards of different sizes – one for light winds and a smaller version for stronger winds. The

HEAT		PLACE	POINTS
16	Finalists	1–8	0.7–8
15	3rd round losers (from heats 13–14)	1–8	9–16
13–14	3rd round losers (if heat 15 is not sailed)	5	9
		6	11
		7	13
		8	15
9–12	2nd round losers	5	17
		6	21
		7	25
		8	29
1–8	1st round losers	5	33
		6	41
		7	49
		8	57
		9	65
		10	73

*Fig 45   The Fanatic Bee, a
production slalom board.*

Fig 46   A slalom skeg.

Length: 281cm.
Width: 59.5cm.
Weight: 8.3kg.
Volume: 115l.

At World Cup events where competitors may use custom equipment, they will often have a quiver of slalom boards for the different conditions. The World Cup boards weigh as little as 6kg, but they are very expensive and very fragile – often not lasting for more than one championship.

Skegs

Slalom skegs are generally smaller than course racing skegs, but very similar in shape and design, and larger than wave skegs. It is important to have a large skeg to help you to rail the board to leeward and improve your upwind performance. A larger skeg also helps to prevent spin out. If your skeg is too big you will find that the board rails over uncontrollably and can also cause excess drag which will slow you down.

larger, light wind boards can become very difficult to keep in the water and gybe as the wind increases. One of the most popular slalom boards used in production slalom board events is the Fanatic Bee which performs well in 11-20kn, but becomes difficult to handle in stronger winds, especially for lighter people – this is because of the relatively large volume of the board (*see* Fig 45).

Below are some technical details about this board:

Nose: single concave.
Mid Section: triconcave.
Tail: double V.
Rails: full rails with tucked under edges, becoming sharper and flatter towards the tail.

Fig 47   A forfin.

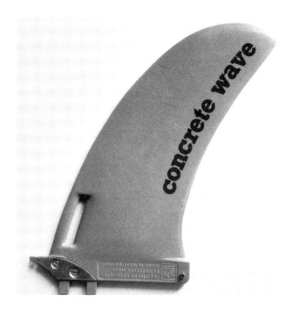

Fig 48   A window fin.

Spin Out

Another way to stop spin out is to try using a skeg with a forfin or a window (*see* Figs 47 and 48).

The only disadvantage with forfins or window skegs is that they can cause a little more drag than a standard skeg. However if it is a case of either getting around the course or spinning out all the time – try a forfin or a window!

Rigs

The rigs used for slalom are the same as those used for course racing. Racers prefer to use the camber-induced sails which are stable and give them good acceleration out of the gybes. Normally a racer would choose a sail for a slalom board one size smaller than for course racing.

Footstraps

The footstraps on your slalom board should be in a similar position to the back set of your course racing footstraps. Use only one set of straps to save weight.

SLALOM RACING TECHNIQUES

Mast Foot Position

It is vital to have your mast foot in the right position when sailing slalom boards. You should have the mast foot as far back as possible, but if you cannot pull the sail in properly with your back hand, move the mast foot further forwards until you can. You will find that the bigger the sail you use, the further forward your mast foot will have to go because of the longer boom. Just a couple of centimetres more can make a big difference to the way your board sails.

Starting

A good start in a slalom race is vital. You should hit the line at top speed at exactly the right time – if you are early you will be disqualified unless you circle and cross the line again – if you are late you will leave yourself with a lot to catch up. To be sure of a good start you must work out a starting strategy in advance.

1. The simplest method is to find yourself a marker buoy in the water approximately 25m before the start line (see Fig 49). You can then time how long it takes to sail from this point to hit the start line. It is important to have a watch with a large readout and easy-to-press buttons.
2. Another method, if you are unable to find any marker buoys, is this:
   (a) first, time how long it takes you to complete a gybe;

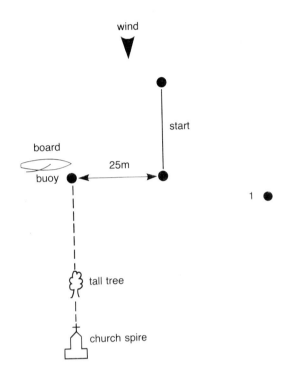

Fig 49   Simple method for slalom
race start.

(b) subtract this time from 60 seconds and then divide the result by two. For example, if it took you 10 seconds to gybe, you will have 50 seconds left, 50 ÷ 2 = 25 seconds;
(c) approach the start boat from the course side with just over one minute to go before the start. Judge your run so that you pass the start boat to windward with exactly one minute to go. Continue reaching away from the start line for exactly 25 seconds, then gybe and sail at full speed to the line which you should hit at full speed at exactly the right time if your calculations were correct (see Fig 50 over the page).

Waterstarting

Most slalom boards need to be waterstarted. Some can be uphauled, but waterstarting is a lot easier and quicker if there is enough wind.

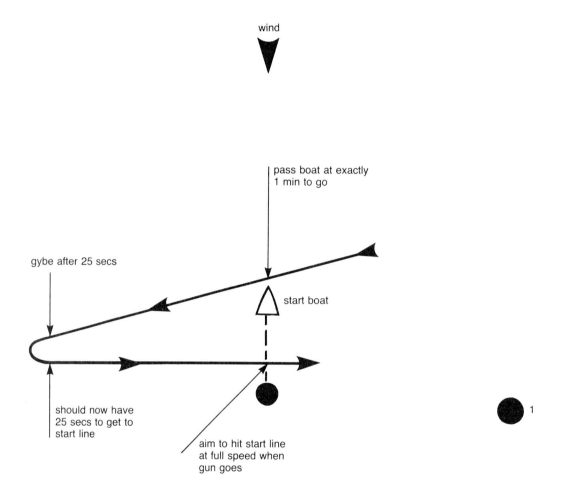

wind

pass boat at exactly
1 min to go

gybe after 25 secs

start boat

should now have
25 secs to get to
start line

aim to hit start line
at full speed when
gun goes

1

Fig 50   Method for approaching slalom race start at full speed.

It is best to learn waterstarting in shallow water where you can always stand up and at a venue where there are no strong tides or currents to affect you. Do not use a camber-induced sail to attempt this as they are heavier than most and harder to get out of the water. If your board has a centreboard make sure that it is retracted. You may find that a buoyancy aid will help if you do not like the water very much!

1. Arrange the board and rig in the water so that all is pointing in the right direction, with the nose of the board pointing into the wind and the rig at 90 degrees to it (*see* Fig 51).
2. The first thing to do is get the rig out of the water – this is the hardest part of waterstarting – once you have done this the rest is easy! Hold the mast with your front hand and pull the rig across your body (*see* Fig 52). The aim is to try

Figs 51–6   Waterstarting a slalom board.

Fig 52

Fig 53

Fig 54

Fig 55

Fig 56

to get the wind under the front of the sail. When the wind is strong be careful that the mast does not get pulled out of your hands.

3. Once the rig is out of the water, transfer your hands to the boom. Push down through the boom to get the nose of the board to turn away from the wind (*see* Fig 53).

4. Put your back foot on the board in the front back strap – turn it slightly so that you can lean forwards, tread water with your other foot gradually bearing the board away on to a beam reach and let the rig pull you up out of the water (*see* Figs 54–6).

Practising the Waterstart

As with most windsurfing manoeuvres, it helps to break them down into sections. When learning how to waterstart it is best to treat it as a deep water beach start.

1. Practise getting the rig into the right position as shown in Fig 51. Allow the rig to fall

Fig 57   Here the rig has fallen into the wrong position to waterstart. Lift
the end of the boom up and the wind will flick the sail over into
the required position.

Figs 58–60   Flicking the sail to return the rig to the correct start.

Fig 59

Fig 60

the wrong way round and practise getting it back into the start position for the waterstart (*see* Fig 57).

2. Practise steering the board in the water as with a deep water beach start, putting pressure through the mast foot.

3. Practise holding the rig up out of the water with your arms straight. Try to make the rig do much of the work.

The Light Wind Waterstart

If the wind drops and there is not enough wind to pull you out of the water, you will have to adapt your waterstarting technique.

1. Start with the nose of the board pointing into the wind with the rig at 90 degrees to it as with a normal waterstart. Take hold of the mast with your back hand and swim upwind with your front hand to lift the rig out of the water (*see* Fig 61 on page 56).

2. As the rig clears the water put both hands

55

Figs 61–5   The light wind waterstart.

Fig 62

Fig 63

Fig 64

Fig 65

on the boom and push down to make the front of the board bear away from the wind (*see* Fig 62).

3. Put your front hand below the boom on the mast (Fig 63), slide your front leg on to the board and then your back leg (*see* Fig 64). As the board begins to gain speed it will become more stable so that you can now stand up, but keep holding on to the mast until you are powered up again (*see* Fig 65).

4. Now pump to gain some speed!

The Reaching Stance for Slalom Boards

This is the same as for course racing boards except that you do not have a centreboard or a sliding mast track to alter. Make sure that you are sailing the board flat on the water or even slightly heeled to leeward. Often when the board feels flat it is actually heeled to windward, so push the leeward rail down further than seems necessary – it does not matter if you overdo it to start with as a leeward heel is definitely faster than a windward heel. Make sure that you find a clean path through the waves – the slightest jump will lose you speed. Anticipate the waves and flex your knees to absorb the jump to keep the board on the water. You should keep the board on the water at all times with the least possible amount of wetted surface.

Fig 66   In this photograph you can see how the sail is pulled down to the back of the board to 'close the slot'.

Carve Gybing a Slalom Board

Carve gybing a slalom board is very similar to carve gybing a course racing board but easier!

Figs 67–71   Carve gybing a slalom board.

1. Sail into the gybe with speed, unhook and take your back foot out of the strap, placing it a little further forward on the leeward rail.

2. The board will start to turn much more easily than the larger course racing board, so continue to lean forwards and bend your knees towards the centre of the turn.

3. As soon as the pressure begins to build in your back hand, release the boom and take hold of the mast with that hand. Continue to carve with foot pressure and the rig will pivot around the nose of the board. Take hold of the boom

Fig 68

Fig 69

Fig 70

with your new back hand, take your new front hand from the mast and put it on to the boom. Only change your feet once the rig has pivoted and you are under way in the new direction.

For reaching and carve gybing exercises *see* pages 36–41.

Fig 71

5 Wave Performance

Wave performance is perhaps the most appealing funboard discipline for spectators and the most exhilarating for competitors if the conditions are right. Wave competitions are different from most other forms of windsurfing competitions because the result is decided by a panel of judges. Competitions are run in heats, competitors sailing one against one, with an elimination system to decide the eventual winner. On average each heat lasts eight minutes. Before the start of the heats, the competitors are told of the course area which will be in front of the panel of judges – if you sail outside this area you will not be judged. The competitors in each heat are given a warning signal, a preparatory signal and a start signal – the competitors then have eight minutes to prove themselves to the judges.

Eight minutes is a very short period on the water. It is very important not to spend your time swimming and to make sure that your manoeuvres are fluent, polished and difficult enough to impress the judges. Try to visualise your routine before you go on to the water – it is no good going for the radical manoeuvres if you know you will just end up swimming. It is important to have the right balance of conservatism and radicalism – you don't lose points for being in the water, but you don't gain any either! Try to fill your eight minutes with a good variety of tricks to keep the judges on their toes.

When you hear the result you must just accept it (or celebrate!); there is no point in getting upset with the judges. You can ask to see the score sheets to find out where you won or lost and to work out what you need to practise. The judges will come from a variety of backgrounds which will probably include surfers, journalists, photographers and sponsors.

The heats will be announced well before you go on to the water. Do not be daunted if you are drawn against the world's No 1! Remember that you are both equal at the beginning of the eight minutes and that the pressure on a competitor who is expected to win will be much greater than the pressure on you – have faith in yourself.

STARTING SIGNALS

The starting signals shall be:

(a) warning signal – red flag;
(b) preparatory signal – yellow flag;
(c) starting signal – green flag.

The intervals between the starting signals shall be either 30 or 60 seconds.

For the right of way rules for wave performance *see* Chapter 13.

WAVE PERFORMANCE ELIMINATION CHART

In Fig 72 you can see how the competition is run – the names of all competitors are distributed evenly by lot on the elimination ladder. Competitors then sail against one another in pairs. The winner of each pair advances on the ladder until the eventual winner is determined.

SCORING

The funboard rules state that each judge shall award each competitor up to:

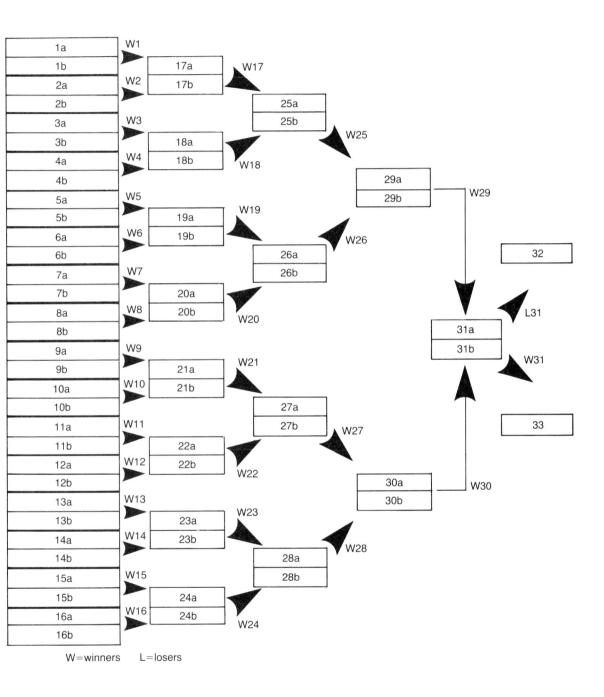

W=winners   L=losers

Fig 72   Wave performance elimination chart.

HEAT		PLACE	POINTS
33	Finalists	1–2	0.7–2
32	5th round losers (from heat 31)	3–4	3–4
31	5th round losers (if heat 32 is not sailed)	3–4	3.5
29–30	4th round losers	5	5
25–28	3rd round losers	9	9
17–24	2nd round losers	17	17
1–16	1st round losers	33	33

(a) 10 points for wave riding;
(b) 10 points for jumping;
(c) 10 points for transitions.

The total varies according to the number of wave rides, jumps and transitions and to the variety and quality of performance. Each judge shall total up the points awarded to each competitor. The competitor with the highest score wins.

Above is a chart of the scoring system used and the points awarded.

WAVE PERFORMANCE EQUIPMENT

Wave Boards

Wave boards are designed to be very manoeuvrable in big waves and strong winds and do not require the rapid acceleration of speed or slalom boards. The manoeuvrability of a wave board is achieved by rounded rails and nose and tail rocker. Most wave boards are between 240 and 260cm long and have a simple underwater shape. Generally, the shorter the board the more manoeuvrable it is, but the more twitchy it will be. The wider the board the slower it will be and the bouncier it will be at high speed. However, wider boards do plane earlier and are more manoeuvrable. Wave boards generally range between 54 and 60cm wide and have to be built to take the force of very high jumps and heavy landings, so they are often the same weight as the larger slalom boards.

Wave Sails

Wave sails tend to have shorter booms than sails for other disciplines, which means you are less likely to catch your boom end in the face of a massive wave. For the same reason there is less sail area under the boom, as this is the first bit of the sail to get caught in the waves. The sails have fewer battens than speed or race sails and no camber inducers, which makes them lighter and more manoeuvrable. Most wave sails have a dual batten system that allows you to choose either full- or half-length battens for the more radical tricks. Some wave sailors sailing in countries where the direction of the wind and waves can be relied on use asymmetric boards designed for jumping and surfing on the same tack – but if the wind comes from the opposite direction you have a problem!

Footstraps for Waves

Again, you should have the minimum of three straps fitted to your board as any others will get in the way. It is important to have a double back strap to give you more control. You will need to keep the straps slightly further apart than for the slalom stance so that you will have more leverage when you are jumping and sailing out through the waves.

Wave Skegs

Wave skegs should be smaller than course or slalom skegs to allow the board to be more

Fig 73 A wave board and sail.

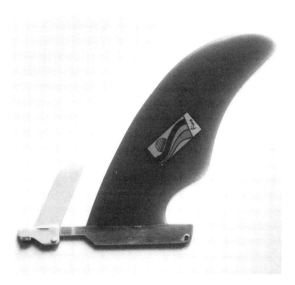

Fig 74 A wave skeg and forfin.

manoeuvrable. Forfins and window fins are very useful on wave boards to help prevent spin out (*see* Fig 74). Some wave boards are fitted with additional smaller skegs called 'thrusters', which help the board to turn and are useful when you are concentrating on your surfing.

THE MANOEUVRES

The basic wave performance manoeuvres are examined later in this chapter. The more advanced tricks are learned by practise, visualisation and a 'go for it' attitude. A typical eight-minute performance at an international event could go like this:

1. The hooter goes, the sailor comes in to the beach and gybes.

2. He clean jumps out through the white water and then makes a forward loop with a good landing.

3. He gybes on to a wave and rides it towards the beach, duck gybes and heads back out to sea.

4. Now is the time for a big jump and the sailor hits a large wave at speed and jumps upside down with a table-top jump.

5. After a good landing the sailor gybes again trying not to get too far away from the judges' eyes, he rides the wave into shore, carving in and out of the white water to make as much use of the wave as possible. The next transition is an aerial gybe which takes him back out through the waves for a long flat jump.

6. As the jump is landed, he gybes immediately on to the face of the next wave, well placed to ride it back to shore. As he approaches the shore it is time to try to impress the judges with a board 360 and then he sails out through the waves again with just enough time for a final upside-down jump as the eight minutes elapse and the heat is over.

An explanation of some of the more advanced manoeuvres follows.

Transitions

The Jump Gybe

1. Sail towards some nice chop and, as you approach it, bear off a little and kick the tail out of the water with your front foot.

2. At the same time, release your back foot out of its strap. The board should then swing a little further through the 180 degree arc you are trying to achieve.

3. Your front foot should be pulled out of its strap just before you land in a clew first position; then flip the rig and you will start sailing on your new tack.

Fig 75   The jump gybe.

The Aerial Gybe

This move should not be tried until you are proficient at the jump gybe.

1. Choose a larger wave than you would for the jump gybe and head at 90 degrees towards it, trying to get as much height as possible. Your aim should be to release the board and send it through a full 180 degrees in the air.

2. As you gain height, release both feet and the board will start to turn. Try to get under the board in the jump and this will help you control the rig and the board in the air (*see* Fig 76). Your old back foot should now be heading for the new front strap on the opposite side of the board.

3. As you come down for the landing, your board will have turned through 180 degrees and your board and sail will be in the clew first position. Try to get your back foot into the back strap and bend your knees ready for the impact of the landing (*see* Fig 77).

4. As you land, flip the rig and sail off on your new tack (*see* Fig 78).

Figs 76–8   The aerial gybe.

Fig 77

Fig 78

The Duck Gybe

The duck gybe is a manoeuvre that looks amazingly good, yet is surprisingly easy to do.

1. Carve the board into a gybe in the usual manner, slide your back hand right to the back of the boom. The shorter the boom, the easier this manoeuvre will be.
2. As the board turns directly downwind and all the pressure goes out of the rig, cross your front hand over your back hand to grab the clew end of the boom.
3. Let go with your old back hand, and pull the boom across your face, back towards the tail of the board. You can then reach through to the new boom and the rig will be ready for the new tack.
4. Grab the new boom with your new front hand, then the back hand. Sheet in and continue to carve the board around on to its new course.
5. Finally, you can switch your feet to their new positions. It is very important to remember to keep the board planing throughout the whole manoeuvre.

Fig 79   The duck gybe.

The 360

This is a complete circle carried out on the water, so that you emerge on the same tack as when you started.

1. Go into the turn as if you were going into a carve gybe, with your back foot out of the strap and the front one in its strap. You will need plenty of speed and to keep the sail sheeted in.
2. Continue to hold the rig firm as your speed increases and you carve around. Carve around harder by moving your body-weight into the turn and pushing on the inside rail.
3. Keep all weight on the inner rail as the leech of the sail passes through the eye of the wind.

4. As the sail sets on the opposite side, concentrate on keeping the inside rail down and making the board turn as much as possible. In stronger winds the rig will try to push you back into the water unless you push the rig lower on to the water.
5. By now the board will have lost much of its speed, so it is necessary to take your front foot out of the strap and move your weight further forward while keeping pressure on the inside rail.
6. Now you can rake the rig back and you will see the tail will slide round and complete the last part of the 360. You can now sheet in and sail back on your original tack having successfully performed a complete 360 degree turn.

Figs 80–3   The 360.

Fig 81

Fig 82

Fig 83

The Helicopter Tack

This is a very useful trick to learn because it allows you to tack a short board without stepping around the mast which is very tricky on low volume boards. It is generally a technique used to get back upwind in lighter winds.

1. Take your back foot out and place it in front of the back strap. Take your front foot out as you start heading up into the wind, place it further forward and in towards the centre line of the board. Keep heading the board into the wind and drop your front hand to hold the mast below the boom.
2. Once the board is pointing directly into wind, change tack by pushing the boom with your back hand while raking the rig slightly forward. This will push the nose around on to the new tack. At the same time push the new windward rail down hard by transferring your weight on to the front of your feet. It is important to go straight from having the sail full on one side, to having it full on the other.
3. The important thing to remember is to get the nose of the board around far enough before letting the sail flip.
4. In a good breeze the sail will flip around very fast. You must anticipate this by spinning your body into position for the new tack. This, hopefully, will leave you in the right position to catch the boom, sheet in and sail away.

Figs 84–9   The helicopter tack.

Fig 85

Fig 86

Fig 87

Fig 88

74

Fig 89

Jumping

A Long Jump

1. Take off as you would for chop jumping.
2. When the nose of the board is airborne, pull the rig back a little, sheet in and squat down so that the board levels off rather than going any higher into the air.

A High Jump

Take off as for chop jumping. As soon as you are airborne use your front foot to lift the windward rail, allowing the wind to get under the board and lift it higher. Crouch down, hang on to the boom and use your legs to pull the tail of the board up and under you.

An Upside-Down Jump

Take off as for a chop jump, but try to pick a large wave which will provide you with a good launching ramp. As you take off, lean as far back as you can and pull up your back foot sharply. As the tail lifts, kick the board over your head into the wind and hang on to the boom as the board turns upside-down.

Fig 90   A long jump.

Fig 91   A high jump.

Fig 92 *An upside-down jump.*

The Forward Loop

This manoeuvre is best practised in the perfect conditions of a Force 5 cross-shore wind and waves of 3–5ft.

1. To take off, hit the almost breaking wave face as quickly as you can.
2. Head the board downwind immediately on take off, which will give you the spinning motion required.

3. Now you will find yourself on top of the sail. Keep sheeted in and you will rise further. The sail will back to the wind, at this point, keep leaning forwards as if to push your leading shoulder in front of the mast. The sail will keep rotating and you will drop from above to below the boom.
4. To complete this manoeuvre all you have to do is to maintain your composure and you should hang-glide back down to where you started from!

Figs 93–6   A forward loop.

Fig 94

Fig 95

Fig 96

Wave Riding Manoeuvres

Gybing on to Waves

This is one manoeuvre that looks spectacular, but is surprisingly easy to perform. Gybing on to a wave is actually easier than on flat water, because the forward motion of the wave will help you to keep the board planing.

1. Approach the wave at speed and bear off to commence the gybe three or four board lengths before the wave.
2. As soon as the nose begins to rise up the face, release the back hand while continuing to carve round.
3. Complete the gybe as usual. On a steep wave it is not necessary to pressure the front foot on exit – in fact you may have to step back towards the tail to prevent the nose from diving.

Fig 97   Gybing on to the face of a wave.

Fig 98   A cutback.

The Cutback

This is a sharp turn made at the top of a wave which takes you down the front of the wave to the point where it is breaking.

1. As you reach the top of the wave, shift your weight to the back of the windward rail and sheet in.
2. As you turn, transfer your weight towards the front of the board and you will ride quickly down the front of the wave.

The Bottom Turn

This is a sharp turn made at the bottom of a wave. As you sail down the face of the wave on a broad reach, bear away from the wind as if you were about to gybe, leaning into the turn and putting your weight on the inner rail. Sheet out and keep the rig forwards as you travel along the bottom of the wave.

Fig 99   A bottom turn.

AN INTRODUCTION TO WAVE JUMPING

Wave jumping forms the basis of all wave manoeuvres and despite the elastic repertoire of tricks being invented, can still be guaranteed to impress the crowds.

You will need a board under 300cm, or smaller. In fact, the easiest boards to sail in waves are approximately 265cm long, although your choice of board depends on your size and the conditions.

1. Choose a venue with safe and small waves – no bigger than 3ft.

2. The ideal wind conditions should be cross-shore – 20kn.

3. Select a wave with a steep peak.

4. Approach your wave with speed.

5. Aim for a peaked section of the wave downwind, or just ahead of you.

6. Unhook yourself from your harness and bring your body into a more upright stance.

7. As you go up the front of the wave, head the nose of the board into the wind, lean back and kick up with your front leg. (Heading the nose of the board into the wind allows the wind to get under the board and helps to lift it.)

8. Pull the rig over the top of your body but keep it fully powered. Lean back and push out

83

Figs 100–2   Wave jumping sequence.

Fig 101

Fig 102

and up with your front foot to gain maximum lift. As the board reaches maximum height, level the board off by picking up your heels. Allow the nose of the board to be swung around by the wind so that you are pointing downwind.

9. As you start to come down, it is time to think about landing. Flat landings are easiest but are not so good for the board after a high jump, so it is best to practise tail first landings, which are the safest.

10. To land tail first, lean back and sheet in a little – this will prepare the board to hit the water at the right angle.

11. As you hit the water, depower the sail momentarily, and most importantly, bend your knees to absorb the shock of landing. If all the force of the landing is taken by the skeg you will spin out.

12. As you land, throw your weight forwards, if you find that you are spinning out, pump your board with your legs to pull the tail of the board back under your body.

HARNESSES

Many wave sailors use waist and chest harnesses, which they feel allow them more movement when they are attempting radical tricks. Wave sailors tend not to load their harnesses with such large forces, as they tend not to use such large sails as in the other disciplines.

Fig 103   A chest harness used for wave sailing.

6 Speed Sailing

Speed sailing is the purest competitive form of windsurfing. Anyone who is competitive has probably experienced the urge to try to go faster than the sailor next to them. There are speed sailing competitions for any level of competitor from the club racer to World Championship racers. Speed sailing is probably one of the simplest forms of competition within windsurfing. There are no awkward turns or tactical knowledge required – all you have to do is hang on and make your board go as fast as possible. Speed trials that you may have read about in the magazines are normally held at national or international events on the well-known courses with sophisticated timing devices. However, the simple enjoyment of speed sailing can be experienced on any Sunday afternoon as you drag race your fellow club members from one side of the lake to the other.

Speed sailing on boards first became popular as a form of competition in 1977 when Dirk Thys won the 'A' Class division at the Weymouth speed trials on a Windglider with a speed of 17.10kn ('A' Class is the under 10sq m class). The class had always previously been won by sailing craft, so the yachting fraternity were not too keen on the influx of boards, but could do little to prevent them. The event at Weymouth had previously been dominated by variations of traditional sailing boats, mostly home-built by eccentric enthusiasts. In the following years, the numbers of windsurfers wishing to enter this event multiplied to such an extent that eventually entry had to be limited. The short board revolution changed the design of both boards and rigs and now the equipment used at speed events hardly bears any resemblance to the original Windglider. You can see the difference in Fig 104.

As the demand for places at events has increased, more venues for speed trials have been found.

WHAT MAKES A GOOD SPEED SAILING COURSE?

The characteristics of a good speed trial course are a strong wind, flat water and a 500m run that can be sailed at between 115 and 130 degrees to the wind. This may seem a very broad angle to sail at, but as the sailors accelerate, the apparent wind swings further around

Fig 104   The large board is a Windglider which was originally used in speed trials; the smaller board is the type of board now used.

in front of them, so that they end up pointing further away from the wind. (Some courses are smaller than 500m but the times achieved on these cannot be officially ratified as world records.) The favourite courses of the speed sailors are the man-made courses: there are two such courses at the time of writing, but it is likely there will be many more built over the next few years. The advantage of these courses is that they can be built at any angle and can be made very narrow to try to eliminate chop.

Les Saintes Maries de la Mer in Southern France

The ditch which has been built here is 25m wide and 800m long, in an area famous for its mistral winds. This is where Eric Beale broke the world record in 1988 with a speed of 40.48kn. (There is another man-made ditch in France at Fos sur Mer.)

Fig 105 Eric Beale on the trench at Les Saintes Maries de la Mer.

Sotavento in Fuerteventura

This is where Pascal Maka beat the outright world speed sailing record and became the fastest sailing craft in the world with a speed of 38.86kn in July 1986. This record was previously held by 'Crossbow' – a 60ft pencil-thin proa with 1,000sq ft of sail area. A major event is held here in the Canaries every summer, when the wind is at its strongest – the wind here is off shore and is funnelled through the mountains and valleys to create a thermal-assisted venturi effect. The sea is very flat because of the offshore wind and the course area is protected by a sand bar.

Portland Harbour in Weymouth, England

At Portland Harbour the prevailing wind is an offshore southwesterly and the speed sailing competition is held annually during the autumn equinox when strong gales are normally expected. The southwesterly wind blows over a low road and sand bar before entering the harbour. Because of the road and sand bar, the water is normally very flat close to the shore. Weymouth was famous during the early days of speed sailing because of its annual speed week – it was here that the first ratified times were recorded for boards – but, now that other good courses have been discovered, Weymouth is not so popular because of its inconsistent winds and choppy patches of water.

West Kirby Near Liverpool, England

West Kirby has now taken over as the No 1 speed sailing venue in England. There is currently a 250m course and the possibility of a 500m course in the future. Speeds of over 40kn were recorded here in 1988, but they could not be official record-breaking runs as they did not take place on a 500m course. The speed course is on a marine lake, with a concrete wall

Fig 106   The speed course on the marine lake at West Kirby.

surrounding it providing flat water, but a very hard spot for landing! When you are travelling at speed and hit a lull, the danger is that you will luff up violently and hit the wall!

THE WSSR COUNCIL

The organising body for speed sailing is the World Speed Sailing Record Council which is recognised by the IYRU. World speed sailing records may only be established under the jurisdiction of the WSSR Council. The rules of the WSSR state that a 'record in each class shall stand until it has been exceeded by at least two per cent'.

SPEED SAILING EQUIPMENT

Going fast in speed trials is about using the right stance on the right rig and board in the right conditions. At events where the conditions are such that it is not possible to break a record, it is still important to the racers to record the fastest times and win the event, so they need a range of equipment for all conditions.

Speed Boards

Speed boards are very similar in appearance to water skis; very narrow, long, light and stiff (*see* Fig 107). Most world class speed sailors have a quiver of six or seven speed boards to use in the different conditions they may meet. The boards are normally all approximately 280cm long, but vary in width from 11 to 17in. As the wind increases, then smaller boards are used. It is important for a speed sailor to use the smallest board he can, as the larger the board, the more drag there is. He or she will also have a set of boards for choppy conditions, which are of similar size but with a different profile.

Fig 107   Eric Beale and his world record breaking equipment.

The typical profile of a speed board has a single concave in the nose running through to past half-height where it splits into a double concave, flattening out in the last foot of the tail to leave a slight V. There is virtually no rocker in the tail and the nose lift is between 140 and 175mm.

If the board is to be used in choppy conditions – which often happens on speed courses when the wind comes from a direction that it is not supposed to come from – more rocker is needed to make the board more controllable. Flats are needed on the rails in the double concave area, which needs to start further forward with a deeper V throughout its length to give the board better directional stability. The tail should be narrower and the board shape longer to maintain the necessary volume.

Speed Sailing Rigs

Speed sails are specifically designed for high speed reaching, normally camber-induced with up to ten full length battens to maintain a constant and controlled flow shape. It is important to choose the right sized rig for your body weight and the wind strength. Too large a rig can be awkward to handle and the extra weight can deaden your performance. Too small a rig may mean that you never get going! If you are sailing in record-breaking conditions of 35kn or more, you will only need a small quiver of sails – a record-breaking sailor will use sails of 3.5–4.6sq m. However, if you are sailing in lighter winds, you will need a wider range of sails.

Masts and booms need to be light and stiff to

Fig 108 A speed rig.

help maintain the constant flow shape and are generally made of aluminium or carbon fibre.

Speed Sailing Skegs

Skegs are most important areas when sailing such small boards – when you are travelling at high speed the skeg is often the only part in the water! Speed skegs are generally smaller than those used in other disciplines. The sailor should use the smallest sized skeg that his board can be held in the water with, as the larger the skeg, the more drag there will be. The problem with the smaller skegs is that you can spin out easily with them, so use a larger skeg in choppier water. The average size of a speed skeg is 7in for a 17in board in flat water – 8in if the conditions are choppy.

Fig 109 A speed skeg.

The general profile of the skeg is short and wide. It is important to make sure that the skeg is faired into the board with no skeg screws protruding, as this can seriously disrupt the water flow and affect your speed.

Mast Foot Position

Generally, the position of the mast foot is 70in from the tail of the board. This will vary depending on the size of sail that you are using – i.e. further forward for a larger sail and further back for a smaller sail.

Footstraps

The positioning of footstraps is very much a personal decision, but generally it is best to have them as far back as possible. Some manufacturers use skeg box fittings for attachments so you can easily change the position.

Boom Height

Most speed sailors have their booms at just below chin height when they are standing upright on their boards.

Harnesses

Most speed sailors use seat harnesses.

Crash Helmets

With speeds increasing all the time, the risk of injury from collisions with equipment or other sailors is high, so crash helmets should be worn at all times.

STANCE AND TECHNIQUE

Waterstarting

One of the first problems that you may come across on a speed board is waterstarting – it can be very tricky! When you put any weight on the board you will find that it sinks. This is not a problem unless you get your weight in slightly the wrong place when the board will try to pop out of the water in any direction that it can! To overcome the problem, try the following method of waterstarting, remembering that the most important thing is to keep your weight in the right place.

1. Put your back foot in front of the back strap and your front foot in front of the front strap; with equal pressure on both feet, the board will float with its nose just free of the water. If your weight is not over the centre line or if you lean too far forwards or too far back the board will shoot free of the water, leaving you to attempt your waterstart once again!
2. If you keep your balance, the rig will eventually begin to work, driving the board forward just beneath the surface. Once the nose breaks through you will rapidly accelerate.

Stance

Once you are travelling at speed, concentrate on your stance. Stand in an upright position and twist your body so that your shoulders are parallel to the centre line of the board. This has the effect of straightening your back leg so that you apply weight more evenly on both feet and straighten your back arm, to pull the end of the boom nearer to the centre line of the board.

When you are hit by a gust, instead of letting out with your back hand try to bear away to increase your speed and make use of the wind (see Fig 105, which shows Eric Beale at speed).

Speed boards are very easy to sail on flat water, but they are not so easy to sail on choppy water where they tend to spin out and try to throw you in all directions. Crash hats and big fins are needed.

In these conditions, it is much harder to maintain this perfect speed sailor's stance; it is very easy to be catapulted when you are attempting it. You may find that you have to hang down further under the rig so that your weight is taken more by the sail than the board – this allows the board to skim over the surface better without catching a rail.

Gybing

Gybing a speed board is very difficult, especially in choppy water, because of the minimal rocker common in speed boards. A good speed board gybe requires constant foot pressure and lots of practice to maintain control throughout the turn.

Exercise for Speed Sailing

When practising for speed sailing, try always to sail against someone else so that you push yourself. It is easy to sail on your own and convince yourself that you are going fast! When you sail against somebody else of similar speed, you know how fast you are really going.

PREPARATION AND STRATEGY

Good preparation in speed sailing can play a major part in achieving a record-breaking run. speed sailing is all about being on the water when the biggest gust of the day hits the course. You have to be ready to be on the water whenever the conditions look good. Make sure that you have enough interchangeable rigs, harness lines and UJs ready for the expected conditions. You should not be rush-

ing around trying to find your gear as everybody else is screaming up and down in the best wind of the day. Try to be on the water as much as possible so that you stand more chance than your competitors of finding that big gust!

Sail Numbers

Make sure that your sail numbers are big and clearly visible, this way you are more likely to get every run recorded. If you have dark-coloured numbers on a dark sail your numbers will not be visible. Stick your numbers on to a large square of white fablon or number material and then stick this on to your sail.

Starting

Make sure you understand the starting procedure fully. Often you will not be timed at events if you start among a bunch and your sail numbers cannot be clearly seen. A starting procedure often used at events is the following: a large buoy is placed about 100m before the starting transit; all intending starters must approach past this buoy; no waterstarts, no gybing and no overtaking are allowed in this last 100m. A faster board must gybe out and restart. Another small mark is placed about 30m from the start transit and no more than one competitor is allowed on this final stretch at any one time.

For more information about sail numbers and starting procedures see page 173–4 of Chapter 13.

7 One Design and Development Class Racing

There is another side of racing apart from the funboard disciplines of course racing, slalom, wave and speed which are all sailed on boards designed for at least 11kn of wind. There are many classes that sail in 5kn of wind and above, on equipment especially designed for these lighter wind conditions. The classes raced are Windsurfer, Mistral, Lechner, Division I and Division II. Windsurfer, Mistral and Lechner are all 'one design' classes, which means that everybody has to sail on exactly the same equipment. Division I and II are 'development' classes and there are class rules which have to be obeyed, but boards and sails can be modified within these rules to allow new ideas to be tried. The class rules control basic outline and weight of the board and size of the sail.

ONE DESIGN RACING

One design racing was the original form of windsurfing. The first board to be invented was the original Windsurfer in 1967 and everybody who windsurfed throughout the world sailed exactly the same board with exactly the same sail. This allowed for very fair competition as it was always the best sailor who won, not the best equipment. As windsurfing developed and multitudes of different boards became available, one design was destined to lose some of its popularity. In its time it saw some of the most popular world championships, with over 500 competitors from around the world competing at the 1983 World Championships in Sardinia.

This is not to say that there are no longer one design racing competitions. Both Mistral and Windsurfer one design classes are still raced throughout the world. As already mentioned, one design racing has the benefit of offering truly fair racing. It also offers a cheap form of competition as you only need one board and one sail, unlike funboard sailing which almost requires a trailer to carry equipment to events!

However, one design racing does have its drawbacks – the volume of the board and designated sail size will normally favour sailors of a certain weight in most wind strengths. If you are very heavy, you will probably find that you are not competitive in Windsurfer or Mistral classes. You would probably be better off competing in the funboard classes where you can choose a board with more volume and a larger sail. The one design classes are raced in separate weight categories to try to overcome these problems.

Another drawback is that one design equipment has to stay the same and cannot be developed, so it becomes very quickly outdated.

DEVELOPMENT CLASSES

Division I and Division II are both development classes where there are outline measurement rules which have to be conformed to, for both sails and boards, but there is enough room for new designs to be developed. Unlike the one design classes, most sailors use different makes

Fig 110   *The original Windsurfer, designed by Hoyle Schweitzer.*

of sails and boards although they will all be the same size. In development class racing the sailor has to pay much more attention to his equipment – the winner will be a combination of the best windsurfer on the best equipment. Development racing is generally more expensive than one design racing because you are always trying to acquire the fastest equipment.

THE BOARDS

The Original Windsurfer

This was designed by Hoyle Schweitzer and Jim Drake in 1967 and has been sailed all over the world since then. An updated version is still raced internationally.

The Windsurfer one design board is made of polyurethane so that it is very durable and excellent for freestyle as it has no sharp edges. It is raced with a 5.6sq m sail which is particularly suitable for beginners and lightweights. The Olympic triangular course is sailed at events and no pumping is allowed. The Windsurfer is a very popular board for team racing events.

Mistral One Design

Mistral have tried to overcome the problem of outdated one design boards by changing their one design board as soon as it begins to be dated. They offer a discounted new class board to class members so that competitors can change over easily. The only problem is that the market is often flooded with out-of-date Mistrals!

The first Mistral one design board was the Mistral Superlight, which was replaced by the Mistral SST in 1985 and has now been succeeded by the Mistral One Design board.

The Mistral One Design board is made of a polystyrene core wrapped in fibreglass with an

Fig 111   A Mistral one design board.

ABS coating. It is raced with the Mistral 6.3 Progress line rig which is not camber-induced.

The course sailed is the 'M' course used at funboard events, although the finish is often at the windward mark so an extra leg is sailed. In some countries pumping is allowed in all wind conditions (*see* page 172). Mistral have an annual World and European Championship and also supply the boards for the Youth and Women's World Championships.

The Lechner

This is also a one design board. It developed from the Division II class and has been chosen as the board for the 1988 and 1992 Olympics. The Lechner will be discussed more fully in Chapter 9.

Division I

Division I was originally introduced to provide racing for flat boards which it was hoped would be easier to sail and more popular than Division II boards. The international growth of this class has been slow and is currently only popular in England where the first Division I World Championships was held at Pentewan Sands in Cornwall in 1987. In fact, Division I has been one of the most popular racing classes in England in the late 1980s, with both production and custom boards competing and performing well. The Mistral SST has proved a good Division I board in mid to strong winds, while custom boards made specifically to Division I rules (looking like Division II boards) have dominated in the lighter winds.

Fig 112   A Division I board being sailed on the rail.

The most successful custom Division I boards are built with a polystyrene core and epoxy skin, to the minimum weight of 17kg with sliding mast tracks and footstraps. They sail just like funboards in winds over 11kn but also perform well in lighter air.

Sailors are limited to using two sails; the biggest cannot be more than 6sq m. The sailors all race together but the results are separated into light, heavy and ladies' classes. The course sailed is an 'M' course. Pumping is strongly policed and is *not* allowed.

Division II

This was the Europeans' answer to the original Windsurfer class racing which was strong in the United States, but not so popular elsewhere. Division II rules were made for racing on any board which could not be raced as a Windsurfer. Division II has always been a very popular class in Europe, especially in France. The fastest boards developed are round in shape and resemble canoes in appearance; they are very fast upwind, but not so quick downwind. They have over 350l of volume which is the reason that they are very quick in light winds, but their size gives manufacturers a difficult task in trying to build to the minimum weight rule of 18kg. Most manufacturers use a hollow sandwich construction based on a PVC foam core. The original sail size for these boards was 6.3sq m, but the rules now allow 7.3sq m.

When Division II was first introduced, it was very much the 'Formula 1' of windsurfing and carried an image which has now switched to the funboard side of the sport with works' teams and manufacturer's sponsorship. To the average sailor, Division II boards are hard to control and unstable, but once a little time has been spent on the board, it performs like a thoroughbred racing machine. It is this quality which has led to the Lechner Division II board being chosen as the Olympic board for both the 1988 and 1992 Olympic games. It is this Olympic status which keeps the Division II class alive in most countries. However, in France, Division II racing is still very popular and keeps everybody on the water and racing when there is not enough wind for their funboards. The type of course sailed is either an Olympic triangle course or an 'M' course.

LIGHT WIND RACING TECHNIQUES

These boards are sailed in the same way as funboards when it is windy but light winds need different techniques.

Railing

To improve a board's upwind performance in light winds it should be sailed with the windward rail lifting slightly from the water. To do this, position the mast foot so that it is in the centre of the track and try to get all your weight off the board and on to the rig by adopting a 'low bum' position and hanging off the boom with straight arms. At the same time push away from you with your back foot on the centreboard head and put your front foot on the rail of the board. Keep trying to make the board rail, and as soon as the windward rail has lifted, try and get both feet on to the windward edge of the board. Be careful not to rail the board over at such an angle that the leeward edge drags in the water and slows you down.

Light Wind Reaching

If you are sailing on a close reach you can again improve your speed by railing your board. Make sure that your centreboard is fully down and follow the above procedure. Do not sail too close to the wind and whenever there is a gust try to bear away to increase your speed. You should be bearing away in the gusts and heading up in the lulls, but don't travel too far off course!

Fig 113   Once the board is on its edge, stand with both feet on the windward rail.

Light Wind Gybing

The best gybe in light winds is the flare gybe. To do this, make sure that your centreboard is down as you approach the mark. With this gybe you spin around very quickly so make sure that you don't gybe too early and miss the mark altogether! When you want to turn, stand as far back as possible and with your outside foot put all your weight on the outside rail. The board will spin around very quickly and as it does, allow the rig to flip and move forwards to stop the board swinging any further into the wind.

Practice Exercise for
Light Wind Gybing and Tacking

The standard slalom course (*see* Fig 43) is an excellent way to practise your light wind gybing and tacking techniques – with a friend or not.

Figs 114–18   The flare gybe.

Fig 115

Fig 116

Fig 117

Fig 118

Pumping

This is the term used to describe the continuous movement of the rig to help increase board speed. In some races and classes pumping is allowed in all wind and sea conditions. Good pumping is very effective while bad pumping uses a lot of energy and doesn't get you very far!

How to Pump in No Wind

It is most difficult to pump in no wind but this is when it is most effective. In absolutely no wind you can propel your board by rowing the rig from side to side. It is tricky to get the rhythm started, but as soon as the board starts to gain speed it becomes much easier. Stand over the centre line of the board as if you were on a run and row the rig as if it were an oar. You may find that if the wind fills in slightly from another direction you will have to gybe to accommodate it.

Fig 119   Rowing the sail from side to side in light winds.

Light Wind Pumping

As the wind increases you will find that you have to change your pumping technique. On a run or very broad reach you can stick to the no wind technique, but if you are sailing upwind or on a close reach, you should revert to your normal sailing technique and use a subtler method to pump. Begin the pump by pulling in with your back hand; once you are sheeted in, straighten your front hand to push the mast forward again, let your back hand out and then pull in to begin the process again.

Strong Wind Pumping

In strong winds the most important time to pump is on the reaches. It is vital to pump yourself into good positions on any waves as they can dramatically increase your speed – as you get on to a wave, pump hard so that you can stay on it for longer.

Times When it is Important to Pump During a Race

There are times during a race when it is much more important to pump than others – for example:

1. Getting off the start line – it is very important to pump off the start line until you are in clean air. If you don't, you will be left on your own at the back!
2. Immediately after you have tacked or gybed – after a manoeuvre you have probably lost

101

Figs 120–2   Pumping the sail on a close reach.

Fig 121

Fig 122

speed and to regain this quickly you will have to pump.

3. Getting out of somebody's dirty wind – if you are immediately underneath somebody and need to get out of the position, you should try pumping.

4. On waves – as mentioned previously, it is vital to pump when you are on any sort of waves.

8 Freestyle

'Freestyle' is a term used to describe a discipline of windsurfing which involves the sailor doing tricks on his board. Freestyle windsurfing used to be very popular in the early days when everybody sailed the Windsurfer one design class, but lately freestyle has lost its popularity because the boards which are now manufactured are not so suitable for freestyle. However, freestyling is still lots of fun and is a great light wind alternative to sitting on the beach and moaning about the lack of wind. It's also a great way to use that old high volume board that has been sitting at the end of the garden for the past decade!

Freestyle used to form part of the overall Windsurfer World Championship, with the competitors performing a routine to get an overall result in the championship. A freestyle routine is very similar to a gymnastics routine with the competition being scored by a panel of judges. Nowadays there are few freestyle competitions, but they can provide great entertainment for your club on a summer's day when there is a light wind. *See* Chapter 15 for details. Practising freestyle is also a great way to improve your boardsailing technique – once you have done a pirouette on the rail, gybing will seem a piece of cake!

EQUIPMENT NEEDED

Board

You will need a board with over 200l of volume and a daggerboard. The original Windsurfer is an ideal board for freestyle because it has a durable construction and no sharp edges for you to land on. It is best to do freestyle on a board without footstraps as you will find that they get in the way at the most inappropriate moments!

Sail

The sail should be no bigger than 6.5sq m, as if it is too big it will be too heavy and powerful for sail tricks. Do not use a camber-induced sail.

Weather and Sea Conditions

You will find it easier to learn tricks in flat water and a light wind of between 5 and 12kn.

Clothing

Wear a wetsuit and shoes when learning tricks, which will help to protect you from any collisions with your equipment. Do not wear a harness and remove the harness lines from your booms as they will get in the way.

LEARNING HOW TO PERFORM A TRICK

No matter how good the explanation of a trick, you will not be able to grasp it unless you go about it the right way. First read how to do the trick that you want to learn, and then try to visualise in your mind how you are going to do it. Then take your board on to a sandy or grassy area and remove the skeg and try to do the trick on dry land. This way you can get a feel for what you are supposed to be doing, so that when you go on to the water you already have an idea of where your feet and hands

Fig 123 Practising on land.

should be! When it is time to go on to the water – sail the board into the trick and just as you come into the critical section where you think that you are most likely to fall in, stop the board and visualise how you are going to do the trick without getting wet! Once you are clear in your mind of the actions you are going to make, repeat the trick all the way through without stopping and with a bit of luck you will pull the trick off! If you don't make it, try to work out why not and don't just carry on making the same mistakes again and again. If you are having too many problems with a trick – leave it and go back and try one that you know that you *can* do to build your confidence again. After a while, come back to the one you are having problems with and you will probably do it this time, now your mind is fresh!

Here are some examples of freestyle tricks, with the easier ones described first, followed by the more difficult.

Clew First

This is a simple trick to start with. To get into the position shown in Fig 124 do a simple gybe but instead of letting the rig swing over the front of the board keep hold of it in its original position. You will find that you have to lean the mast towards the back of the board as it turns and move your hands further apart on the boom to keep control of the sail. It will be trying to pull away from you all the time, but try to hold it like this as long as possible. When you can hold it no longer, quickly let go with the hand that is nearest the clew and move your other hand on to the mast. Keep hold of the mast and allow the sail to pivot around the front of the board back into its normal sailing position.

Fig 124 Begin to gybe the board.

105

Fig 125   *Keep hold of the sail, do not allow it to swing.*

Fig 126   *Move your hands further apart on the boom for more control.*

Fig 127   *To keep the board on a controlled course, lean the mast towards the back of the board.*

Sitting on the Board

This is the lazy way to sail! Position your board on a beam reach, move your feet a little further apart than usual, start to bend at the knees and move your front hand down on to the mast just below the boom, move your back hand to the foot of the sail (*see* Fig 128). Sit on the board with your legs crossed to keep them out of the water (you will have a lot of drag and steerage problems if your legs are in the water). Keep the sail sheeted in with your back hand. You may find that you have to lean the mast forwards slightly to keep the board sailing correctly. To return to a standing position, come back up on to your feet and move your hands quickly back on to the boom.

Lying on the Board

This is an even lazier way to sail! Position your board on a run downwind with the wind

Fig 128   Sitting on the board.

directly behind it. Stand with your feet on either side of the centreboard, bend your knees and move your front hand down on to the mast below the boom and your back hand to the foot of the sail. Drop on to your knees as soon as you can – this will make you more stable. While continuing to keep the sail powered and the board moving, bring your legs out from underneath you and sit with your feet pointing forwards. Now lie back on the board and you may find that you have to move your hands further down the sail and mast (*see* Fig 129).

Once you have reached this position try bringing your feet up on to the boom! Continue to lie down on the board, bring your legs up between your arms and try to hook the tops of your feet over the top of the boom – your legs will need to be quite far apart. Pull down with your feet so that you are taking the pressure of the rig and let go with your hands (*see* Fig 130).

To get out of this position, return your hands to the mast and sail, put your feet back on to the board, bring your feet back underneath you, stand up and return your hands to the normal sailing position. It is important that the board always points directly downwind or there will be too much pressure in the rig and the board will swing up into the wind and you will get wet!

Fig 129   Lying on the board.

Fig 130   Steering the board with your feet.

Sailing Inside the Booms

Sail on a close reach in the normal sailing position. Move your front hand from the boom to the mast, just below the boom cut-out. Bend your knees and pull the booms towards you slightly, remove your back hand from the boom and duck underneath so that you are now inside the booms, lean back on the boom immediately and stretch your back arm out along the boom to help you balance (*see* Fig 131). Don't lean back too much or else you will be in the water! The amount you lean back against the boom now controls how much you sheet the sail in. Be careful not to bear away too much, remember you have to lean the rig back slightly to keep the board pointing up into the wind.

The easiest way to exit from this position is to move your front hand back on to the mast below the boom, bend your knees and quickly duck underneath the booms and back into your normal sailing position.

The Sail Spin

Start on a reach, walk around the front of the mast so that you are pushing against the back of the sail as in Fig 132 and if the board starts to luff into wind, lean the mast forwards, while if it starts to bear away, lean the mast back. Your front foot should be just in front of the mast and your back foot just in front of the centre-board case, both over the centre line of the board. To begin the trick, push down on the sail with your back hand, as the sail spins, move your feet back to the normal sailing position. Keep pushing with your back hand until the clew of the sail passes through the eye of the wind, let go with your back hand and allow the sail to complete its spin around your front hand, then put your old back hand on to the new front hand position on the new tack. This is shown in Figs 132–6.

Fig 131 *Sailing inside the booms.*

Figs 132–6 *The sail spin.*

Fig 133

Fig 134

110

Fig 135

Fig 136

The Head Dip

There are two versions of this trick, one for light winds and the other for stronger winds.

The Light Wind Head Dip

Sail on a close reach, move your front hand down on to the mast below the boom and your back hand to the foot of the sail as shown below. Bend your knees and sit on the windward side of the board with your legs lying across the board, bending your knees so that your feet don't drag in the water (*see* Fig 137). Arch your neck so that your head touches the water.

This is the light wind head dip. Return to the normal sailing position by reversing this procedure.

The Stronger Wind Head Dip

When the wind is stronger you can do the head dip from the standing position. Sail on a close reach, bend your knees, stretch your arms, arch your back and pull the rig slightly over on top of you (*see* Fig 138). Your head should now be just touching the top of the water, but if it is not, try again aiming to get your head a little closer to the water every time and keep on trying until it does.

Fig 137   Light wind head dip.

Fig 138   Head dip in stronger winds.

Sailing Back to Sail

Start this trick by sailing on a close hauled course. You now have to get around the mast to the other side of the sail, so take your front hand from the boom and put it on to the mast, take your back hand from the boom and put that on the mast, now take your front hand from the mast and step around the mast (*see* Fig 139). Change hands again with the mast so that it is again held by your front hand, and now that you are on the other side of the sail, move your back foot towards the back of the board and lean back into the sail. If the board starts to bear away, lean the rig towards the back of the board and if it heads up into wind, lean the rig towards the front of the board (*see* Figs 139–41 for the sequence).

Figs 139–41   Sailing back to sail.

Fig 140

Fig 141

Sailing Back to Sail Inside of the Booms

This is a very easy progression from the previous trick. Once you are in a stable position leaning back into the sail, just duck under the booms, and lean back against the sail, again holding the booms loosely with your hands. This is much more comfortable than leaning back against the booms.

Sailing Inside Out

Start by sailing on a close hauled course. You now have to turn around so that you are facing away from the sail – this is done in one quick move! Turn in an anti-clockwise direction. Move your back hand from the boom on to the mast just below the cut-out. Move your front hand to the position that your back hand has just left. At the same time spin your feet around so that they have changed over positions (*see* Fig 144). You will now be standing with your back to the sail, with the sail trying to pull you over. You should now arch your body forwards so that your knees, pelvis and chest are leaning outboard (*see* Fig 145). To get out of this position, spin back around in a reverse of the procedure above (*see* Figs 142–5 for the sequence).

Pirouette

The pirouette is one of the more elegant tricks and is very easy to perform once you have mastered it. Sail on a close reach and luff the sail slightly, at the same time tilting the rig to windward. This part of the trick is very important, you must place the rig cleanly and well balanced into the wind so that when you let go

Figs 142–5 *Sailing inside out.*

Fig 143

Fig 144

Fig 145

Fig 146 *The pirouette.*

it will be ready for you to catch when you have completed your pirouette. Spin clockwise on the ball of your back foot, kicking off with your front foot, and as you spin around you will see that the rig is ready to collect. Do not rush your spin, you will find that you have enough time to do a double pirouette – give it a try!

The Spin Gybe

This is a very neat manoeuvre that can brighten up the conventional gybes. As the sail passes over the front of the board your aim is to spin around and catch the sail as it arrives on the opposite side. Do everything that you would for a conventional gybe, but once you have let go of the rig with your back hand, put your back hand on the mast and spin around on the ball of your foot, catching the mast with your front hand. By now the sail should be ready to collect on the new gybe (*see* Figs 147–50 for the sequence).

Figs 147–50   The spin gybe.

Fig 148

Fig 149

Fig 150

Fig 152

Figs 151–5   The spin tack.

The Spin Tack

Once you have mastered the pirouette you will not have much difficulty with the spin tack. It is a trick that can be done in any condition and looks really impressisve. Begin to sail into a conventional tack and once you are heading into the wind, release the boom with your back hand and spin 180 degrees on your foot. Place your free foot in front of the mast, release the boom with your front hand and put your free back hand back on to the mast. Continue your spin on the foot in front of the mast and as you spin, tilt the sail forward and grab the boom, sheeting in and sailing off (*see* Figs 151–5 for the sequence).

Fig 153

Fig 154

Fig 155

The Railride

This is a very impressive trick and forms the basis for many freestyle moves. The trick consists of sailing your board on its edge with your feet on the rail or daggerboard. It can be quite a painful trick to learn if your board has sharp edges – you should wear a wetsuit with legs or some kind of good shin protection. To learn this trick you need 10–12kn of wind. Sail along on a close reach and put your back foot on to the leeward side of the deck, transfer your weight to this foot and hang off the booms. Now squat down, slip your forward foot under the windward rail and flip the board on to its side (*see* Fig 156). Your weight will transfer to your front shin as you lift your back foot on to the rail. This is a one foot railride (*see* Fig 157). Pull down again on the booms to lift your forward foot on to the rail. This is a two foot railride (*see* Fig 158). A word of caution – do make sure that your mast foot is held

Fig 156 *Getting the board on to the rail.*

119

Fig 157 *Sailing with one foot on the rail.*

Fig 158 *Sailing with both feet on the rail.*

securely in the board during this trick as there will be a lot of pressure put on it.

The Duck Tack

This is very similar to the conventional tack performed by yachtsmen on all types of sailing craft, but on a windsurfer it is considerably more difficult to tack by passing under the boom! To perform this trick you don't need too much wind – try it in 5kn to start with. Head up into the wind as with a normal tack until you are just past head to wind, then tilt the luffing sail forwards into the eye of the wind. Slide your forward hand back along the boom as the foot of the sail rises to a height convenient for you to step under. As you step under, pull the

rig back and away from you. Quickly take hold of the boom on the new tack and push the rig forwards to bear away (*see* Fig 159).

Stepping Out Through the Booms

This is a trick that can be used in a routine or as an impressive dismount. Start by sailing on a run or a broad reach. Duck under the booms so that you are sailing inside them and then turn around so that you are facing out. Be sure to keep the board sailing downwind. Push the back end of the booms down towards the board and step over them quickly with your back leg first, pivot at the same time so that your back leg becomes your new front leg and you are now facing the sail in your normal sailing

Fig 159 The duck tack.

Fig 160   Sailing downwind inside
of the booms.

Fig 161   Stepping out of the
booms.

position. Now you will find yourself at the back end of the board with the tail sinking, move quickly towards the front of the board and resume your sailing position (*see* Figs 160 and 161 for the sequence). If you are using this trick as a dismount at the end of your routine, put all your weight on the tail of the board as you step out of the booms to send the front of the board flying into the air – the only way out of this is to get wet!

The Somersault
Through the Booms

This trick is another good dismount. If you pull this trick off successfully you will score highly, but the likelihood is that you won't, so it makes

an impressive dismount! All but the most advanced windsurfers should wear a crash helmet so as not to crack their head on the board. Sail on a beam reach, lean towards the rig and begin your somersault by lifting your feet into the air, trying to stay as close to the boom as possible throughout the turn (*see* Fig 162), try to land with both feet on the board and resume your sailing position. This is a difficult trick to do but is certainly very impressive if you succeed.

DEVELOPING A ROUTINE

Most freestyle competitions require a routine that lasts for approximately three minutes. A good routine will consist of flowing manoeuvres

Fig 162 Somersault through the booms.

Figs 163–6   Moving from the spin gybe
to sailing inside out.

Fig 164

Fig 165

Fig 166

with one trick running into the next. You will find that with practice you will be able to link tricks without returning to your normal sailing position in between them. You will probably find that you will be making up a few new tricks of your own as well! At the end of the routine you will need an impressive dismount – at this stage you are probably going to get very wet! There are many more tricks besides the ones described above, but these will give you a good basis from which to work. Here is an example of a typical linking manoeuvre used in freestyle routines.

Spin Gybe to Sailing Inside Out

This is a very impressive but easy manoeuvre to link two tricks, and is typical of the kind of move that you should try to develop in order to put together a flowing routine. It is best first attempted in 5-8kn of wind.

Sail as if you were going to do a spin gybe, allowing the board to turn and the sail to flick, but instead of completing your turn, remain facing out, catch the rig behind you on your new tack and push down with your back foot to make the board turn into the wind (*see* Figs 163–6 for the sequence).

TANDEM FREESTYLE

Tandem freestyle means two people on the same board performing tricks together. Competitions are unfortunately rare but it is an excellent way of spending a hot, sunny, windless day. You will need a board with plenty of volume, especially if you or your partner is heavy, in fact the lighter you are the better for tandem freestyle. The variations of tricks possible are endless, but some of the more popular ones are:

1. One sailor standing on the other sailor's shoulders.
2. One sailor standing either side of the sail.
3. One sailor inside the boom, the other outside.
4. Both sailors standing on the rail.

9 The Olympics

Windsurfing received a tremendous boost in November 1980, when the International Yacht Racing Union (IYRU) decided that it should become an Olympic sport, and would be included at the 1984 Olympic games in long Beach, Los Angeles, USA. This was probably the most rapid rise to Olympic status that any sport has made. In the case of windsurfing it only took thirteen years from its conception in 1967 to full Olympic status. After a successful Olympics in 1984, windsurfing was again chosen as an Olympic sport for 1988 and 1992.

THE 1984 OLYMPICS

The board chosen for the Olympics in 1984 was the Windglider, which was manufactured in West Germany by Fred Ostermann. It already had a strong following in Europe with the World and European Championships attracting many sailors. The Windglider was chosen over other existing boards because Ostermann had presented a sound case to the IYRU. He had already established a strong class association in many countries and this maintained the strong one design principles of the IYRU. Construction was relatively straightforward in glass-reinforced plastic, enabling the board to be built world-wide. Ostermann was also willing to license builders and provide tooling to build his board. The other existing international classes of Mistral and Windsurfer lost out to the Windglider for these reasons and also because the Olympic games would not allow weight categories. Unlike Mistral and Windsurfer boards, due to its higher volume the Windglider has better tolerance to different body-weights and therefore does not need to be raced in weight divisions.

The Olympic decision prompted windsurfers from all over the world to begin training to try to win windsurfing's first gold medal. An early favourite was Holland's Stephan Van den Berg, who, as reigning World and European Champion, had already proved that he was at home on this particular board. In fact, by 1981 he had won five world titles in various classes. The Windglider class was different to all other classes as harnesses were banned, which made the racing a test of tactical ability and a test of fitness, thus making it a true Olympic sport.

As the class progressed towards the Olympics, the sport of windsurfing began to develop rapidly, both on and off the water. The result of this was that Ostermann was taken over by the French board manufacturer BIC. This resulted in a new rig being developed by various manufacturers specifically to be used on the Windglider at the Olympic event. The rig contract was awarded to North Sails in Germany, who produced a new alloy mast matched to a sail built from Norlam laminated sail cloth. The consequent increase in mast stiffness allowed sailors to control their rigs in higher wind speeds and also gave heavier sailors more power to offset their weight disadvantage.

The Olympic racing was held in the huge Long Beach harbour with beats of 0.9 nautical miles. The Olympic race was sailed without weight groups – so there was just one Olympic Champion. However, windsurfing had been chosen as both an Olympic sport and a demonstration event: the only time that a sport has been picked for the two categories in its first year. This was a reflection of the speed at which the sport had grown prior to the games.

Fig 167   The Olympic Windglider racing.

The demonstration event was sailed on Windsurfer boards, provided by Hoyle Schweitzer, the true father of windsurfing. As Los Angeles was Schweitzer's home, this was a fitting tribute. Unlike the Windglider event the demonstration event was sailed in separate classes for men and women, and also in four different disciplines. These were course racing, freestyle, long distance and slalom, chosen to highlight the different aspects of windsurfing. Competitors in the demonstration events did not receive Olympic medals.

THE FIRST
WINDSURFING OLYMPICS

On 31 July 1984, forty competitors from forty different countries started the first race in a seven race series to decide windsurfing's first gold medal. Favourite, after winning his fifth consecutive World Championship was Stephan Van den Berg, but it was West Germany's Dirk Meyer who won the first race. He actually crossed the finish line in second place behind Frenchman Guildas Guillerot, who was subsequently disqualified for pumping.

This series was dominated by much lighter winds than had been expected, normally at that time of year in Los Angeles the winds would build from 11–22kn during the afternoon due to the strong thermal effect. The lighter winds favoured lightweight Scott Steele of the USA, who was considerably lighter than Van den Berg and most of the other sailors. Before the event most sailors had tried to lose as much weight as possible.

After five of the seven races Scott Steele had a

5-point lead over Stephan Van den Berg, but as the wind increased in the sixth race Van den Berg regained the lead with a second place as Steele faltered with a ninth. The final race could have seen a tremendous fight between Van den Berg and Steele for the gold. However, the wind steadily increased before the race and Steele must have seen the gold medal slipping away. This was the windiest race of the series and Van den Berg cruised to an impressive victory and the gold medal. Steele hung on to his silver medal position despite a determined effort from the New Zealander Bruce Kendall who missed it by just one point.

WINDGLIDER CLASS RESULTS — 1984 OLYMPICS

GOLD	Stephan Van den Berg	Holland
SILVER	Scott Steele	USA
BRONZE	Bruce Kendall	New Zealand

THE 1988 OLYMPICS

The board chosen for the 1988 Olympic games was the Lechner A 390 with a 6.3sq m sail. The course was the same as in 1984 with triangle racing being the only Olympic discipline. This time harnesses were allowed which made things a little easier. All of the equipment was again provided by the organising committee.

As you can see from Fig 168 the Lechner has a large amount of volume – 350l. This makes it an unbeatable racing machine in light winds, but as the wind increases they are difficult to sail due to the large volume and unstable rounded hull shape.

Unlike the Windglider Olympic class where one sailor dominated, the 1988 Olympic class was dominated by one country – France. They had had virtual dominance in the class in the years leading up to 1988 with such sailors as

Fig 168   The Lechner railing upwind.

Herve Piegelin, Michel Quintin and Robert Nagy. With over 3,000 Division II sailors in France it was no surprise that their sailors had repeatedly won World and European titles. This strong home fleet had allowed the French to develop good sailors due to the competition, but it had also allowed them to win through their technology. Many designers and builders of boards work in France and the sails, boards, masts and booms were nearly all of French origin so France had a double advantage.

The French finally picked Robert Nagy as their Olympic hope, as the more experienced sailor who had won past World and European championships. However, he must have known that there were two major factors against him at the 1988 Olympics.

First, there was the equipment. At previous regattas the French had used their own equipment which was more advanced than that used by the rest of the world. At the Olympics they would have to use equipment supplied which would be identical to that used by everyone else.

His second problem was the expected conditions in Korea, Nagy was the most experienced sailor in France but he was not the quickest sailor in a breeze. In 1987 at the World Championships in Canada he had been beaten by both Michel Quintin and Herve Piegelin of France in windy conditions. At the pre-Olympics in 1987, Korea had proved itself to be a windy venue – Nagy had won this regattta but there *were* some big names missing from the entry list. Nagy also had the added pressure of the French press believing that he could not fail to win a gold medal for their country.

The line-up for the Olympics in 1988 included the 1984 bronze medallist, Bruce Kendall from New Zealand; the 1984 silver medallist Scott Steele was also present, but this time in a coaching role with Mike Gebhart from the USA. Other front runners were Bart Verschoor from Holland, Richard Myerscough from Canada, Paco Wirz from Italy, Jan Bonga from Switzerland and the little-known Jan Boersma from the Dutch Antilles who had shown impressive speed in the practice races.

Race 1 started with an increasing wind and saw lightweight sailors desperately hanging on while weight paid, and the heavier sailors, Boersma, Bonga and then Kendall crossed the finishing line first. The race favourite Nagy crossed in fifteenth place. Nagy again had a bad time in Race 2, and it was looking as though he had definitely thrown away the gold medal, when he finished in a disappointing fourteenth place – he now had an unexpected uphill struggle in front of him. However, he managed to bounce back in Race 3 and was in contention for first place fighting a battle in the lighter winds with New Zealander Bruce Kendall. It was Kendall who crossed the finishing line first, having won a tactical battle with Nagy. Kendall had now established himself as leader of the regatta having been consistent in all conditions.

Race 5 was more like a destruction derby than close tactical racing. Winds gusted to 35kn and seas built up against the strong 2kn current. Boersma looked at ease as he sailed around the course while most of the others struggled, with Kendall finishing in eighth position. Only fifteen boards finished the course while twenty-five retired including Nagy who claimed that his equipment had failed – he asked for the 'yacht materially prejudiced' rule to be applied to his case, which meant that he would receive average points for the race. At first this was refused, but the protest jury reopened the case stating that the equipment failure had not been due to his neglect. He was awarded average points which meant that he still had a chance of winning a medal.

Race 6 was held in 12–16kn of wind, Bruce Kendall stamped his mastery on this one. He led from start to finish, slowly pulling away to win the race comfortably, and with that the gold medal was already his with a day to spare!

The final race was to decide silver and bronze from among five sailors: Boersma; Gebhart; Wirz; Nagy; and Verschoor. As the wind built up Boersma, the heavy wind expert, looked to be the favourite. In the 30kn of wind he finished second to Thomas Wallner of Austria to win silver and his country's only Olympic medal! Gebhart from the USA hung on to fourth place to clinch the bronze medal.

FINAL RESULTS — 1988 OLYMPICS

GOLD	Bruce Kendall	New Zealand
SILVER	Jan Boersma	Dutch Antilles
BRONZE	Mike Gebhart	USA

THE 1992 OLYMPICS

In November 1988 the IYRU voted that women should have their own division and race at Barcelona in their own windsurfing class. After much debate, the Lechner A 390 was chosen for both the men's and women's classes. The one design rig will be decided closer to the games, but at present the Division II rig rules apply to the Lechner which prescribe a 7.3sq m camber–induced sail.

Techniques for Sailing the Lechner A 390

The Lechner and Division II boards are both very different to sail than other boards. Here are a few tips to help you master the art of sailing these racing machines.

Sailing Upwind

To sail a Division II board quickly upwind you have to sail it on its rail. This is not difficult as long as there is some wind. In very light winds you will have to work hard to get the board on to the rail to start with, but once it is there it is easy to hold the position. To get it on the rail hang from the boom so that you are transferring your weight from the windward rail to the rig, and push with your back foot against the centreboard top. You may find that it helps to bring the mast track back slightly in light winds as this helps the board to rail a bit more.

Once you have the board sailing on the rail, stand with both feet on the windward rail. Take care not to rail the board too much or the leeward edge will drag in the water and slow you down.

As the wind increases you may find that the board is trying to rail too much. If this happens retract the centreboard a little.

Reaching in Light Winds

Pull the mast track back a little, but keep the centreboard down to give you more stability. If the reach is tight, try to rail the board as you were doing upwind.

Reaching in Strong Winds

Retract the centreboard fully and pull the mast track to the rear of the track. Use the rear footstraps and sail the board as if you were sailing a funboard.

The Run

This is the downwind leg of the course. In very light winds you can sail straight down this leg with your centreboard in a mid-way position. As soon as the wind increases to planing conditions, it is quicker to sail the run in a series of broad reaches instead of sailing straight down it.

Gybing

In light winds flare gybe the board with the centreboard down. In planing conditions carve gybe the board with the centreboard retracted. You will find that you have to get right to the back of the board and keep your arms straight so the rig remains upright.

10 Equipment Preparation

It is no longer good enough just to be the best sailor in the world; to win major championships now you also have to be the most well-prepared sailor in the world. If you have not put in the work on your equipment, you will never win an important event. So often you will hear excuses from sailors such as 'I was leading until my slot gasket came off' or 'My harness lines came undone'. When you are in the lead it is not the time to remember that you have forgotten to do that work on your centreboard which makes it impossible to retract at that moment!

At all levels, races are won and lost on mistakes. The person who makes the fewest mistakes will win the race. Even world champions make some mistakes, but they will not make as many as the people behind them. Windsurfing is a complex sport and it is very rare for anyone to complete an event without making a single mistake, i.e. rounding a mark badly, or stumbling in a gybe (although some may never admit it!).

Many mistakes are technique-orientated and can only be eradicated by practice. However, there are other mistakes that can easily be avoided such as a mast track which takes ages to move because it is stiff, or a skeg that is not fitted properly and causes the board to keep spinning out. These mistakes can all be avoided by spending time before the event working on your equipment. In the following pages each piece of equipment is considered and ways of looking after them to help improve your performance are suggested.

THE HULL

The hull is the underside of the board which is in the water most of the time. It is very important for this part of the board to have a low drag factor and so be very efficient through the water. It is not a good idea to have a hull covered in holes and scratches from where it has been dragged up the beach. To improve the hull, first wash it down with a household cleanser like Jif and water, and then fill any deep scratches or holes with the gel coat that you can buy from most marine or hardware shops. If a hole has pierced the skin of the board, consult a specialist board repairer and make sure that the hole is dry before you attempt to repair it. Once the gel coat has dried, sand the repaired area with wet-and-dry sandpaper, start with a course grade such as 200 and work down to 600. Do not use a smoother grade than 600, or you will start to polish the board, which is not the finish you require. Make sure that you use plenty of water with the sandpaper to prevent you from scratching the board unnecessarily and to give you a better finish. Use a sanding block so that you sand evenly and do not create dents in your board. Once you have filled all the scratches, sand the entire surface of the hull with 600 grade wet-and-dry sandpaper, again using plenty of water.

If you have just bought a brand new hull you will probably notice that it has a very bright finish – this looks very pretty in the shops but it is not very fast! If you are planning on taking your racing seriously you will have to sand down your new hull. Use wet-and-dry sandpaper, start with 240 grade, then 400 and then finally 600 – again using plenty of water. Hulls are always in need of attention, but don't become too vigorous as the hull is only covered in a thin gel coat or paint layer which can be sanded through very easily.

You should check your board after every trip on the water to make sure that there are no holes appearing from a bump on the start line or collision with the mark. If you leave a hole for too long, you will get water into your board and it will delaminate, get heavier and be beyond repair.

Another good way to look after your board is to always use a board cover. A thin nylon cover will protect your board from road dirt, stone chips and roof-rack scrapes when you are travelling. When you are travelling by air it is best to use a padded board cover.

THE DECK

The deck is the area of the board above the hull on which you stand. One of the most important things about the deck is to have a good non-slip surface on it. Most boards now come with adequate non-slip but if you have an old board you may find that a better non-slip surface saves you from quite a few falls.

Wax

This is the easiest form of non-slip to apply and can be brought in packs from most windsurfing shops. Just rub it on in the areas which are slippery. It is important to buy a wax that is suitable for the climate you will be using the board in. Some waxes are made for cold climates and melt as soon as the sun shines for too long on them. Other waxes are very difficult to apply in cold weather. You will find that wax gradually wears off and needs replacing. If you put too many layers of wax on top of each other, the wax will not work – remove it by rinsing in very hot water then reapply.

Paint and Spray on Non-Slips

These are available from most windsurfing shops and can be applied easily. If your new non-slip deck is too abrasive, sand it down with coarse sandpaper until it is comfortable.

If both these methods fail try taking your board to a specialist board repairer who should be able to suggest a suitable non-slip for you.

Again, it is important to keep the deck clean with a board cover to prevent the non-slip from being scraped away by roof-racks, etc. or being clogged up with road dust.

THE CENTREBOARD

As with the hull, it is very important that the centreboard and skeg do not cause any excess drag; it is also very important that the centreboard fits properly in its case. First, put your

Fig 169 Adjusting the centreboard fixing device.

Fig 170 Taping up the head of the centreboard.

board on its side and fit the centreboard; when the centreboard is in its vertical position, it should be quite solid in the board and not flopping from one side of the case to the other. You will probably have an adjustment system at the top of the centreboard casing which you can tighten to make the centreboard fit better (*see* Fig 169). If you have an old board without this system try packing the head of the centreboard out with a fabric tape or gluing thin battens to the inside of the centreboard case (*see* Fig 170). Now you must make sure that the centreboard retracts properly, it has to be easy enough to adjust with your foot, but not so loose that it falls out of the case on reaches when it is supposed to be retracted. If this happens the board will suddenly spin up into wind, throwing you into the water! Again, if your case has adjustment screws, this is easy to sort out – if it has not you will again have to tape the centreboard head correctly. You may

find that after your board has been used a lot, you will have to check the centreboard again in case the tensioning systems have worn. If you tend to retract your centreboard upwind when it is windy, it is useful to mark your centreboard head with the position that you use it in – this allows you to get your centreboard to that position in the middle of a race without any time-wasting trial and error. Mark the centreboard with a line (*see* Fig 171).

As mentioned earlier your centreboard needs looking after in a similar way to your hull. If any scratches or holes appear, fill them and sand your centreboard regularly with 600 grade wet-and-dry sandpaper. Keep your centreboard in a bag to prevent it from getting knocked about in the back of the car or in the garage. If you use a smaller centreboard for windy weather make sure that it also fits and retracts properly, so that it is ready for action when you need it.

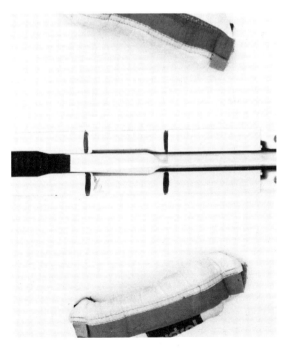

Fig 171 Marking up the centreboard case.

Fig 172   A slot gasket.

The Slot Gasket

This is the length of rubber, cloth or mylar that covers the entrance to your centreboard case on the hull of the board (*see* Fig 172). If you do not have a slot gasket you will have noticed on a reach that you have lots of water forcing up through the centreboard case – this does not help your speed! A gasket can increase your speed by approximatley fifteen per cent – it prevents water from entering the centreboard case from the hull side of the board and thus increases the board's efficiency through the water. If you do not have a gasket on your board here is how to make your own. Take great care when you are fitting it because a gasket that starts to peel off in the middle of a race is slower than not having one at all.

1. To put on your own gasket you will need a strip of thick mylar gasket three times the length of your centreboard slot and 2–3in wide, a strong contact adhesive such as Evostick or Thixofix, a sharp pair of scissors, tape, a marker pen and pencil.
2. Place the board hull side up on a dry surface. Measure the distance from 3in in front of the centreboard slot to 3in behind it. Cut two lengths of mylar to this length. Cut the front ends at forty-five degree angles so that they will come together in a point (*see* Fig 173).
3. Place the strips of mylar along the centre line of the slot, starting from 3in in front of the opening to 3in behind it. The two straight edges over the centre line of the slot should meet exactly together, with no overlaps and no gaps. Hold the mylar in place by taping it down on the outside edges, lightly draw around

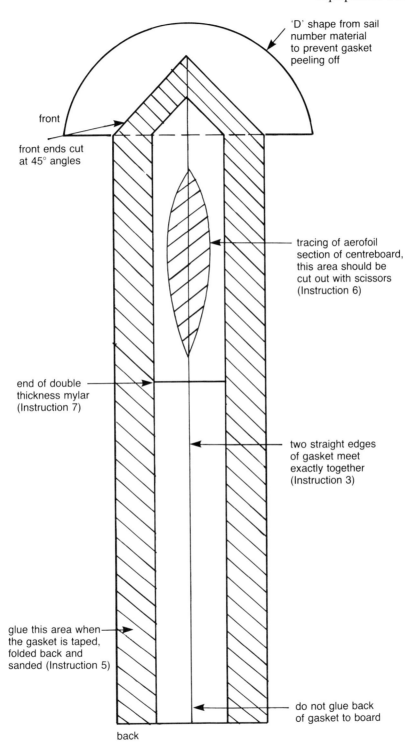

'D' shape from sail
number material
to prevent gasket
peeling off

front

front ends cut
at 45° angles

tracing of aerofoil
section of centreboard,
this area should be
cut out with scissors
(Instruction 6)

end of double
thickness mylar
(Instruction 7)

two straight edges
of gasket meet
exactly together
(Instruction 3)

glue this area when
the gasket is taped,
folded back and
sanded (Instruction 5)

do not glue back
of gasket to board

back

Fig 173   Making your own slot gasket.

the front and back of the gasket with a pencil. Once you have marked the position, fold the gasket back on the tape to get it out of the way so that you can glue underneath.

4. Lightly sand the area of the board between the folded back gasket and the edge of the slot. At the front of the gasket, sand from the pencil marks to 1in in towards the slot along the same angles that you have drawn. At the back, sand until you get to the back pencil line.

5. Use a good contact adhesive such as mentioned above. Follow the manufacturer's instructions and apply the glue to the sanded area around the slot and the section of the mylar which will come into contact with the hull when it is folded down into position. You should not glue all of the mylar, as part of it will be over the slot and not stuck to the hull.

Wait for the specified time and then fold the mylar strips into place so that both pieces meet together exactly and press them down firmly to make sure they stick well. Follow the glue instructions carefully. Once the mylar is stuck, remove any excess glue and tape with solvents. If you are racing at club level go straight to instruction Stage 7. If you race at championship level, read on:

6. After half an hour carefully place the centreboard so that it is in a vertical position. Using a felt tip pen draw on to the mylar around where the centreboard is distorting it. Retract the centreboard and you should be left with the aerofoil section of the centreboard drawn on to the mylar (see Fig 173).

Carefully cut this section out with sharp scissors. Put the centreboard back into its vertical position and you will see that the mylar now fits perfectly against the centreboard with no distortions. Retract the centreboard.

7. To make a double thickness of mylar along the front section of the gasket, you need to measure the length from the front of the gasket to 1in aft of the centreboard cut-out which you have just made. Cut two pieces of mylar to this length and repeat stages 1–5, then, just before you glue, sand the bottom layer of mylar to help

the two layers to stick well together. Remove tape and any excess glue with solvents.

8. To help prevent the gasket from peeling off, cut a large D shape from sail number material and stick it over the front of the gasket (see Fig 174).

If you have bought a board recently it should be fitted with a gasket. It is important to maintain this properly; check it for any tears or signs of coming away from the board which could lead to problems in the middle of a race. Always repair or replace a gasket if it is looking suspect – this is too important to take any risks with when you are racing. If you are trying out your gasket on dry land with your centreboard make sure the gasket and board are well lubricated with water or you may tear the gasket. Always wash the gasket out well after you have been out on your board.

THE SKEG

This is a much-neglected part of the board when it comes to preparation. It is vital that the skeg does not cause excess drag. The skeg must also fit firmly into the skeg box, as, when you are travelling at high speed, it is often only the skeg which is left in the water. If it is loose in the board it will not be able to take the pressure demanded of it and will cause the board to spin out. The aerofoil shape of the skeg is also important for speed, if there are nicks in it from the last time you hit a sand bank you will be giving away vital seconds. Use the same system for caring for and repairing your skeg as you do for your centreboard. If you take your skeg out and change it over, always keep it in a bag to stop it from getting scratched or broken.

To enable your skeg to fit tightly in the skeg box, you will need a sharp knife and a piece of thin mylar (or plastic carrier).

1. Place your board on grass or similar surface, deck down. Cut a piece of mylar so that it is large enough to wrap around the bottom of

Fig 174   Fitting the skeg tightly.

the skeg and up both sides (*see* Fig 174).

2. Decide on the position of the skeg in the box and put the back end of the skeg into the box at this point. Wrap the mylar around the base of the skeg which is going into the box and push down on the skeg, taking care that the mylar stays in the right position.

3. If the skeg feels solid, screw it down. If it is still loose repeat stage 2.

Most new boards are supplied with plastic shims that you can push in to your skeg box to fill in the excess space at either end of your skeg. This makes the board much more efficient through the water (*see* Figs 175 and 176). If your skeg box will not take these plastic shims then you can fill the spaces in the box with polyurethane foam which can be pushed below the surface and then covered with a filler such as plastic padding.

MAST TRACKS

It is very important to have a mast track that works well. There is nothing worse than struggling all the way down the reach trying to pull your mast track back while everybody else overtakes you! After every race make sure that your mast track is working properly before you put your board away. Wash the track out and lubricate it if it is sticking. Use Surflube or a similar Teflon-based spray, taking care that it does not spill on to the deck or you will have a very slippery surface.

Most mast tracks are now calibrated (*see* Fig 177). If you have an early board without calibrations – it is a good idea to mark yours up. Use a numbering system of 1–10 marked along the side of the track at equal intervals. It is very useful to know the position you should be

Fig 175   The Plastic shims which fit into the skeg box.

Fig 176   The shims fitted in the skeg box to give a smooth finish.

Fig 177   A calibrated mast track.

sliding your mast foot to in the heat of the moment. It is also useful when you are practising and find you have a good speed, you can then check and see what positions you have been using so you can easily reproduce this speed.

Short Boards

You probably will not have sliding tracks on your short boards but it is still important to mark the positions that you prefer to use in particular conditions or with certain sail sizes.

FOOTSTRAPS

Check your footstraps carefully. Make sure that they are screwed in properly and not about

to break out from the board. Also make sure that they are the correct size and remember that you will need different sizes if you have just changed from wearing boots to bare feet!

RIGS

If you are going to race, one of the first things you should do is put sail numbers on your sails. This is best done when your sails are new, clean and dry. How to put your sail numbers on is covered in Chapter 1.

Rigging Up

Rigging up sails at events is always a most time-consuming and laborious task, especially if you have to waste time working out your boom height and length and how many extensions you need on your masts – often there are at least six sails to rig. It is very easy to work out a coding system that can be used on sails to save time when you are rigging up.

1. Pick a windless day and rig all your sails up on the correct masts, booms and extensions as you would use them at an event.
2. Use a waterproof pen to code each sail.
3. Adjustable booms normally come in three sizes – wave, slalom and race. Use W for wave, S for slalom and R for race.
4. Use the letter X for mast extension.
5. If you are using adjustable mast extensions and booms, you should be able to work out a system of counting the number of adjustments in from the end that you are using, i.e. if you are using a wave boom on a sail which needs to be set on a length which is six notches in from the end, then it would be coded as W.
6. Do the same for mast extensions.
7. To make sure that you are always putting your boom at the right height, use a measuring stick. Cut a batten to a height that you like to have your boom at and put this against the mast before attaching your booms (*see* Fig 178).

*Fig 178   Measuring the boom
          height with a batten.*

Fig 179   Coding your sails for fast rigging.

8. The coding that you label each sail with should look like Fig 179. This sail needs a race boom on position No 5 with a fixed length mast extension. If you are using adjustable mast extensions you should also code the sail for them.

Now that you have a good coding system, rigging will be much easier and quicker and guarantees that you will not be making any mistakes with the wrong boom height etc.

Tips for Rigging Up
a Camber-Induced Sail

Camber-induced sails are very powerful and fast when rigged correctly, but if they are rigged badly they can be very hard to control. Here are a few tips that should help you with correct rigging.

1. When you are sliding your mast into the luff tube make sure that the cambers slot on to the mast correctly (*see* Fig 180).
2. Tension the downhaul enough for the sail to be taut.
3. Clip your boom on at the correct height.
4. Over-tension your outhaul – this will make the cambers easier to locate and the downhaul easier to tension (*see* Fig 181).
5. Re-tension the downhaul (*see* Fig 182).
6. Make sure that the cambers are located properly and that you have sufficient batten tension.
7. Now let off your outhaul until you have the required camber in your sail (*see* Fig 183).

Fig 180 *A camber inducer.*

Fig 181 *Tensioning the outhaul.*

Fig 182   Tensioning the downhaul.

Fig 183   Releasing the outhaul to put more shape into the sail.

142

HARNESSES, LINES AND POSITIONS

If your harness or lines break in the middle of a race, you are going to have problems.

1. First, check that nothing is about to break, that your harness is secure at the points that take the strain, and that the straps are not worn and that the hook is not cracked.
2. Check the lines and holders, make sure that the lines are not going to break and that the holders are not tearing.
3. Make sure that your harness lines are the right length. Some people use adjustable harness lines so that they can be shortened upwind when they are overpowered and lengthened on the reaches (*see* Fig 184 and 185). If your harness lines are hard to change from boom to boom, make sure that you have enough harness lines for each rig.

4. Make sure that the harness line holders are in the right position on the boom. You can mark this position on to the boom or take measurements. Remember that as it gets windier you will need to move the lines further back along the boom.

BOOMS

Take care of your booms:

1. Always wash your booms out after use, especially if you have been using them near sand. Take the ends off and hose out the tubes to clean them thoroughly. If you do not do this you will find that you cannot adjust your boom and it will eventually corrode and break.
2. Check all rivets and end fittings to make sure that there are no weak points – do this especially if you have just had a few catapult falls.

Fig 184   The harness lines in their longest position.

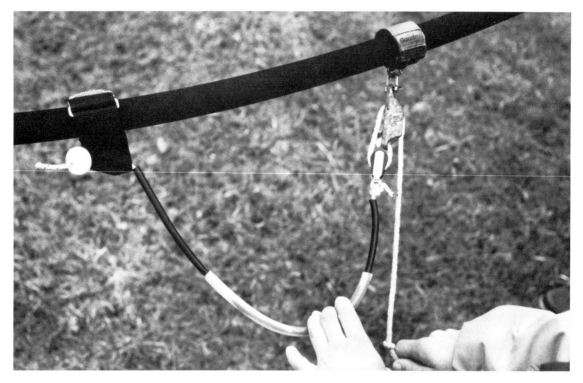

*Fig 185   The harness lines in their shortest position. They were
shortened by pulling the rope.*

MASTS

Regularly check your masts for cracks around the boom area and for bends (*see* Fig 186).

ADJUSTABLE SYSTEMS

In the past, both adjustable outhaul and down-haul systems have been used to aid sail control. Now that the stability of sails has improved, it is not so necessary to have these systems. The shape of most camber-induced sails is now controlled by downhaul rather than outhaul, but because of the tension required to pull on the downhaul with the new sails, a downhaul system has yet to be developed that is powerful enough. An adjustable outhaul system can be fitted and is useful if you are taking part in a long race with a big sail – if you become overpowered, you can flatten the sail by tensioning the outhaul.

The Adjustable Outhaul System

This system is adjusted by ropes attached to cleats on either side of the boom just aft of the back hand position (*see* Fig 187).

BAGS

As mentioned previously, using bags for your equipment will save it from many unnecessary knocks and scrapes and lengthen its life. There are basically two sorts of bag available, either padded or non-padded. The padded version is great for travelling by air or train where you

Fig 186   *Checking the mast for cracks and bends.*

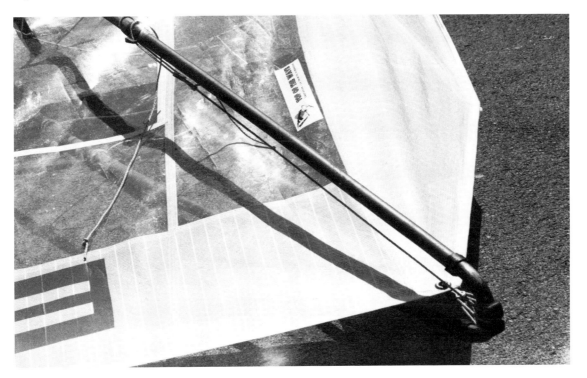

Fig 187   *An adjustable outhaul system.*

Fig 188   Skeg and centreboard bags.

Fig 189   The Shorebreak bag in the middle is not padded and is ideal
for protecting your board from road dirt and stone chips while
travelling by car or trailer. The Art padded bag gives extra
protection when travelling by plane, etc.

*Fig 190 Boards are tied on top of each other on the roof with a line to
tie the front of the boards to the front of the bumper to
prevent them from lifting off.*

need to protect your board. When you are
carrying your board on a roof-rack on the car,
the non-padded version is sufficient as long as
you remember to protect one board from the
other if you are stacking them in a pile. When
you are looking for a cover, remember that you
will probably have to lock your board on to the
car roof, so you will need a hole in the cover to
fit your chain through. Here are some examples of good bags to protect your gear:

1. Mast bag.
2. Skeg and centreboard bags (*see* Fig 188).
3. Board bag (*see* Fig 189).

TRAVELLING WITH
YOUR EQUIPMENT BY CAR

1. Check your roof-rack – make sure that it is
solid and secure.
2. Pad the roof-rack with foam or special
roof-rack pads to prevent it from scratching
your gear.
3. Tie boards down one on top of the other
using roof-rack straps – check that they are not
beginning to wear.
4. If you are travelling long distances use extra
straps in case one breaks.
5. Tie the booms and masts down on top of
the boards.
6. Tie the boards down to the front of the car
to stop them from lifting up and pulling the
roof-rack away from the car.

7. Always check your load regularly during your journey. You could seriously injure someone if a board fell from your car.

TRAVELLING WITH
YOUR WINDSURFER BY AIR

1. Check with your travel agent and/or airline to ensure that your board and masts can go on the flight. Usually it is better if you take a two-piece mast.

2. Pack up your gear well in padded bags. Do not have one piece of luggage that is very heavy as this is more likely to get dropped – try to spread the load around. Don't have too many small pieces as you then stand more chance of losing something.

3. Place packing over any sharp edges such as the ends of masts.

4. Arrive at the check-in desk early. It will be less crowded, the airline staff will be less hassled and have more time for you.

5. Remember to take a roof-rack and straps if you are hiring a car at your destination.

6. A good tip is to take a small board trolley with you, which will save you a lot of carrying at the airports.

11 Fitness

(**IMPORTANT:** Before embarking on any demanding fitness training programme it is advisable to have a medical check-up.)

Windsurfing is not a sport that demands Olympian fitness, but as you progress you will find that the fitter you are the more enjoyable windsurfing becomes. For example, if you are fit you can stay out on the water for longer without getting tired, which means that you will improve faster. You will find that in races you can push yourself harder, because you know that you are fit enough to do it – being fit also gives you a psychological advantage over the opposition. If your muscles are in good shape you are less likely to suffer from windsurfing injuries, which will mean more hours spent on the water and less in the physio department!

Without doubt the best way to keep fit for windsurfing is to windsurf in strong winds day after day, but this is not a possibility for most people. In Chapter 12 an on-land training routine is suggested. One part of which can be done without any equipment and the other for which you will need weights. Besides being generally fit it is also important to be flexible for windsurfing so that you can react to gusts and complete manoeuvres which require a large range of joint and muscle movement. Before and after a training session, on or off the water, it is important to do a series of exercises to warm up and warm down.

THE WARM-UP

Injuries often occur if you make sudden movements when you are cold. Before going windsurfing, or starting your fitness training, do a five minute warm-up programme as suggested below.

1. Loose jogging on the spot with toes remaining in contact with the ground.
2. Chest stretches – feet together, arms raised forwards to stretch up and drop to sides again. Do this four times. (*See* Fig 191.)
3. Side stretches – feet apart, one hand above head and the other reaching as far down to floor as possible on side you are leaning to, lean over and hold to a count of three. Repeat on each side four times. (*See* Fig 192.)
4. Twist – twist to right to a count of three. Repeat four times. Twist to left to a count of three. Repeat four times. (*See* Fig 193.)
5. Back arches – arch backwards to a count of three. Repeat four times. (*See* Fig 194.)
6. Toe reaching – feet together, slide your hands down your shins, press your knees back. Hold for a count of three. Repeat four times. (*See* Fig 195.)
7. Shoulder pressing – arms apart, press backwards for a count of three and release. repeat four times. (*See* Fig 196.)
8. Shoulder stretching – arms stretch up for a count of three and release. Repeat four times. (*See* Fig 197.)
9. Ski bounces – keep seat low and full knee bend on forward and back swings. Repeat four times. (*See* Figs 198–200 for sequence.)
10. Side swings – feet apart. Deep squat on each swing. Repeat four times. (*See* Figs 201–3 for sequence.)
11. Lunges – right leg four times, left leg four times. (*See* Fig 204.)

Fig 191   Chest stretches.

Fig 192   Side stretches.

Fig 193   Twists.

Fig 194   Back arches.

Fig 195 *Toe reaching.*

Fig 196 *Shoulder pressing.*

Fig 197 *Shoulder stretching.*

Figs 198–200 *Ski bounces.*

Fig 199

Fig 200

Figs 201–3 Side swings.

Fig 202

Fig 203

Fig 204 Lunges.

THE COOL-DOWN

Cooling down after exercise assists with the recovery process by preventing a build up of lactic acid and therefore preventing stiffness the following day. It also helps to avoid injuries. The cool-down programme should consist of stretching exercises as illustrated in Nos. 2–11 of the warm-up programme above.

FLEXIBILITY

As already mentioned it is important to be flexible for windsurfing. It is possible to maintain and improve flexibility by regular, gentle stretching exercises. For flexibility exercises to be effective it is important that the end of the range movement be reached and the position held for a few seconds. It is important that stretching exercises are always carried out in a controlled manner, as violent or rapid movement can lead to injury. This flexibility programme should be performed six days per week after windsurfing or training and can be incorporated as part of the cool-down programme.

Flexibility Programme

Foot Extension

Starting Position – sitting on floor with legs together, straight out ahead.
Action – tense thigh muscles, press toes and feet forwards to full extension, count to three and release. Repeat four times. (*See* Fig 205.)

Foot Rotation

Starting Position – as for foot extension.
Action – tense thigh muscles, rotate feet clockwise four times and then anti-clockwise four times. (*See* Fig 206.)

Fig 206   Foot rotation.

Fig 205   Foot extension.

Foot Contraction

Starting Position – as for foot extension.
Action – pull feet and toes towards you, hold for slow count of three and release. Repeat four times. (*See* Fig 207.)

Alternate Leg Raising

Starting Position – lie flat on floor with legs together and straight ahead.
Action – Stretch foot and raise right leg to count of three. Repeat with other leg. Repeat four times with each leg. (*See* Fig 208.)

Fig 207   Foot contraction.

Fig 208   Alternate leg raising.

Knee to Chest Contraction

Starting Position – lie flat on floor with legs together and tensed, straight ahead.
Action – lift knee to chest and keep resting leg tensed. Press knee down to count of three and release. Repeat four times with each leg. (*See* Fig 209.)

Knee Presses

Starting Position – sitting on floor with soles of feet together.
Action – press knees down towards the floor, count to three and release. Repeat four times. (*See* Fig 210.)

Fig 209   Knee to chest contraction.

Fig 210   Knee presses.

Back and Leg Extension

Starting Position – sit upright on floor with legs stretched apart.
Action – slide hands forwards on floor between legs. Keep your legs as far apart as possible and hold tensed. Count to three and release. Repeat four times. (*See* Fig 211.)

Back Extension and Leg Extension With Twist

Starting Position – as for back and leg extension.
Action – reach hands towards left ankle, keeping legs tensed, count to three and release. Do the same for right ankle. Repeat exercise four times on each side. (*See* Fig 212.)

Fig 211   Back and leg extension.

Fig 212   Back and leg extension with twist.

Back Arches

Starting Position – lie face down on floor with hands directly below shoulders.

Action – push up on your hands to arch your back and chest, keep your trunk on the floor. Count for 3 seconds and then release. Repeat four times. (*See* Fig 213.)

Plié

Starting Position – stand with your heels together and legs tensed.

Action – keep feet flat on the floor, lower your trunk by bending your knees and pressing down directly over your feet. Count to three and release. Repeat four times. (*See* Fig 214.)

Fig 213   Back arches.

Fig 214   Plié.

Body Raising

Starting Position – stand with your feet together and flat on the floor with toes pointing forwards.
Action – extend your feet until you are balanced on your toes and have raised your body. Count to three and release. Repeat four times. (*See* Fig 215.)

Lunges

Starting Position – stand with legs apart, turn body sideways, turn front foot to face same way as head. Keep your legs tensed and your arms out to balance you.
Action – lower your body into a lunge position, bending front knee. Count to three and release. Return to starting position and repeat four times on each leg. (*See* Fig 204.)

Shoulder Press

Starting Position – stand up with legs apart and arms straight out at sides.
Action – press arms and shoulders back, keeping arms straight. Count to three and release. Repeat four times. (*See* Fig 196.)

Shoulder Stretch

Starting Position – stand up with legs apart and arms straight up above head.
Action – stretch shoulders and arms upwards to count of three and release. Repeat four times. (*See* Fig 197.)

Backward Stretch

Starting Position – stand up with legs apart, arms above head and bent at elbows.
Action – bend arms and reach down your back as far as possible. Count to three and then release. Repeat four times. (*See* Fig 194.)

Fig 215   Body raising.

Trunk Twists

Starting Position – stand upright with legs apart and hands clasped together behind back.
Action –twist trunk to right to look behind you. Count to three and then release. Repeat on both sides four times. (*See* Fig 193.)

Side Leans

Starting Position – stand upright with legs apart.
Action – place right hand on head and lean over to the left side to reach as far down left leg as possible with left hand. Count to three and release. Repeat four times on both sides. (*See* Fig 192.)

ON-LAND TRAINING WITHOUT WEIGHTS

This sort of training is generally known as circuit training. It improves your muscular endurance and aerobic fitness. It does not need any specialist equipment so it can be done at home or when away at training camps or regattas.

1. Start with your warm-up, *see* pages 149–52.
2. Press-ups.
3. Sit-ups.
4. Squats.
5. Back lifts.
6. Squat thrusts.
7. Step-ups.

To work out the number of repetitions that you should be doing, run through all the exercises recording the number of each exercise that you can perform in a minute. Divide this number by two and record the figure alongside each exercise, this is the number of times you should do each exercise at a time. Each circuit session should consist of three sets of Nos. 1–7. Try to do this session as quickly as possible and record the time the session takes you each time. As your fitness improves you will find the circuits become easier. Every four weeks re-test yourself on the number of each exercise that you can do in a minute and change your programme accordingly.

WEIGHT TRAINING

Before attempting any weight training consult a specialist at your gym so that you know how to perform each exercise properly and the exact weights to use.

When deciding on the weights to use, choose the weight that you can just manage ten repetitions of each exercise with. Record the weights that you are using for each exercise and as your fitness improves try to use heavier weights.

Exercise	No of reps	No of sets
1. BICEPS CURL	[10]	[3]
2. PRESS BEHIND NECK	[10]	[3]
3. HIGH PULLS	[10]	[3]
4. SQUAT	[10]	[3]
5. WRIST CURL	[10]	[3]
6. REVERSE WRIST CURL	[10]	[3]
7. PULL OVERS	[10]	[3]

AEROBIC FITNESS

As mentioned, it is important to have a good level of aerobic fitness. To improve aerobic fitness you have to put your heart under pressure for at least 20 minutes each day – preferably

Fig 216   Off-road cycling for aerobic fitness.

30 minutes. Suggested ways of doing this are:
1. Cycling up hills or off road;
2. Running;
3. Swimming.

PLANNING YOUR FITNESS ROUTINE

It is important to have one day off in every seven, and this should be a complete rest day. Weight training should only be performed three times per week. Circuits, aerobic training and flexibility should be done six times per week. You may find it very helpful to keep a record of your progress. You may find that if you are windsurfing as well as training that you prefer to train on land after windsurfing so you are not too tired on the water.

A Typical Day's Training

1. Get up – eat a biscuit to raise blood sugar level before exercising.
2. Five minute warm-up.
3. Thirty minute run.
4. Work or windsurf.
5. Five minute warm-up.
6. Circuits.
7. Weights.
8. Cool-down.
9. Flexibility.

12 Goal Setting and Training Diary

An important part of the learning process in any sport is correct goal setting. An important goal will give you direction, a sense of purpose, accompanied by enthusiasm and hopefully achievement. First, decide on a long-term goal – probably a year in advance. This has to be a goal that you see to be important – it could be anything from winning the World Championships to just finishing a club race, but whatever the goal it has to be realistic. For example, if you have never competed at national level you are not going to win a World Championship next year. Unrealistic goals lead to disappointment and lack of enthusiasm, but, on the other hand, goals which are too easily achieved will give you no sense of attainment. Once you have decided on your long-term goal you have to set yourself intermediate and short-term goals which will lead you to success in your major goal. Try to select goals which are not dependent on the performance of others, for example, however well you sail you cannot guarantee that you will win, because other people may sail better than you – finishing in the top five is more realistic. Goals do not only have to be performance-related, but can also be aimed at developing new skills.

Here are some examples of goals:

Long-term goal – finishing in top ten in the World Championships.
Intermediate goals –(a) develop speed in all conditions;
(b) improve tactics and rule knowledge;
(c) attend all UK regattas.

Short-term goals – (a) read rules and tactics book;
(b) increase training sessions to two hours per day.

Your short-term, intermediate and long-term goals will obviously have to be revised once they are achieved, but try not to revise them before that!

To record your progress you should keep a training dairy. These are valuable for training both on and off the water – below is an example of the kind of information that you should be keeping and evaluating.

A TRAINING DIARY FOR FITNESS TRAINING

As mentioned in Chapter 11 it is important to keep a record of your training so that you know when it is becoming too easy and you need to step it up. It will also show up days when you have done no training and hopefully make you feel guilty!

Date:
Aerobic training: record length of time taken.
Circuits: record number of reps of each exercise and the time taken to do three sets.
Your body weight:

A TRAINING DIARY
FOR ON-WATER TRAINING

Date:
Wind strength:
Sea state:
Board used:
Sail used:
Over-powered, under-powered:
Race or practice performance:
Comments:

Keeping a record of your on-water training will enable you to analyse the equipment that performed best in the different conditions. It is very useful to have a hand-held wind speed recording instrument so that you can record the wind as you go out on the water and then work out the biggest sized sail you can use in those conditions.

If you have any problems with any equipment (or even with yourself!) whilst out practising or racing, remember to write that down as well. These details will help to remind you if you need to repair something or perhaps do some more practice on certain manoeuvres such as gybing.

13 Rules

If you pick up a copy of the IYRU racing rules your first impression may well be 'How can I learn all this?' The answer is quite simple – you do not need to know all the rules to compete. The reason why there is such a comprehensive set of rules is that, unlike other sports, windsurfing is self-governing and there are no referees. The rule book must therefore cover all possible circumstances. In order to start racing you need to have a grasp of some of the basic rules which you will find at the start of this chapter. As your board handling improves so will the opportunity for confrontations with other windsurfers and suitable rules will be outlined later in the chapter to overcome these situations. Special reference is also given to the rules governing slalom and wave performance, as these differ from the IYRU rules.

We must also mention protests, as this is the main way to learn the rules. Protests take place when an incident has occurred and no one has accepted responsibility; a panel of experienced sailors will listen to the information from each windsurfer and then decide which rule is applicable and who was in the wrong. The person in the wrong will probably be disqualified from the race, but they *will* have learnt a new rule! It is worthwhile taking the time to attend a club protest so that you can see how windsurfing polices itself and you will hopefully learn some new rules. In this way you will very quickly obtain a thorough grasp of the complex rule book. Below is an outline of the order in which a protest hearing is conducted.

PROTEST HEARINGS

Preliminaries

Examine the protest – notify all concerned – call the protest committee.

Hearing

1. Call protestor and protestee.
2. Ask parties whether they object to any members of the race committee.
3. Read out written protest.
4. Enquire whether the protestor tried to inform the protestee that a protest would be lodged.
5. Call on protestor to state complaint.
6. Invite protestee to question protestor. (Questions only.)
7. Invite the protestee to give his account of the incident.
8. Invite protestor to question protestee. (Questions only.)
9. Race committee may question both parties.
10. Invite protestor to call witness to:
    (a) give account of incident;
    (b) be examined by protestor;
    (c) be cross-examined by protestee;
    (d) be questioned by committee.
11. Invite protestee to call witness (plus (a)–(d) of No 10 above).
12. Invite protestor to make final statement.
13. Invite protestee to make final statement.
14. Call on parties to withdraw while committee reaches a decision.
15 Find facts – apply the rules. Return both parties and read out both facts and application of rules and decision.

THE BASIC RULES

The basic racing rules originate from the International Yacht Racing Union (IYRU). These rules are formulated for use by sailors and windsurfers and a copy of your national rules can be obtained from your national windsurfing or sailing authority. To start racing at club level you must have a grasp of at least the five rules which are explained below. These rules have all been devised to help avoid collisions, in fact even if you are in the right but cause serious damage to a windsurfer in the wrong you too will be penalised if you failed to make a reasonable attempt to avoid the collision. It is important to avoid collisions at all costs. This way insurance premiums will also stay lower!

Rule 1

Opposite tacks (IYRU Rule 36). 'A port tack board shall keep clear of a starboard tack board.'

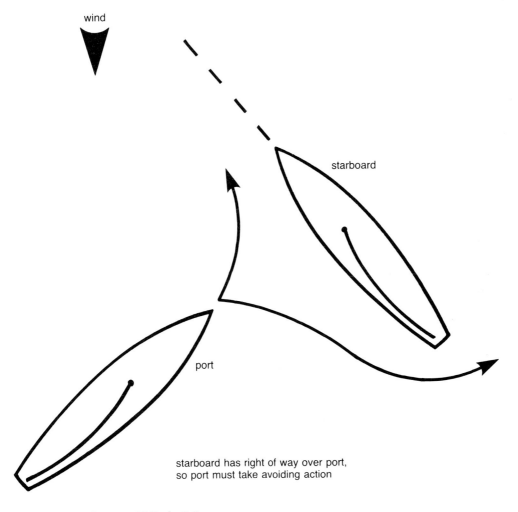

wind

starboard

port

starboard has right of way over port,
so port must take avoiding action

Fig 217 Opposite tacks (IYRU Rule 36).

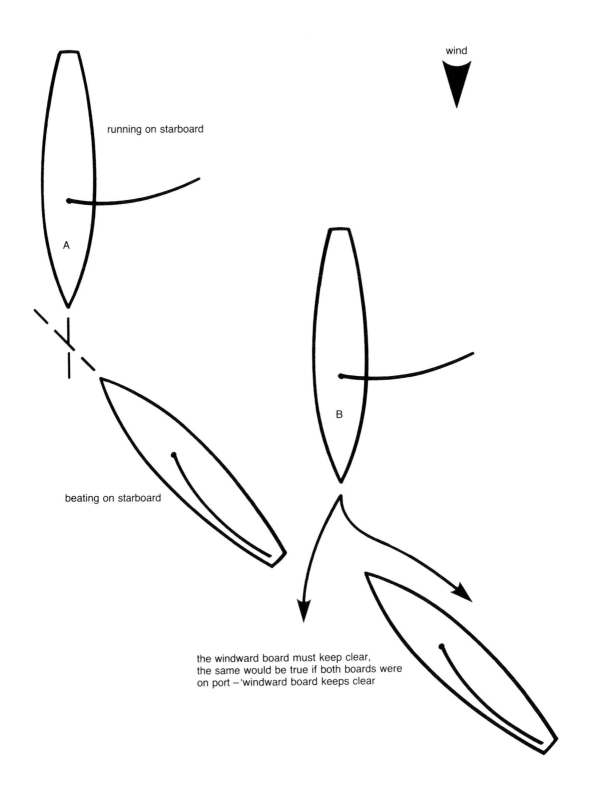

running on starboard

A

wind

B

beating on starboard

the windward board must keep clear,
the same would be true if both boards were
on port – 'windward board keeps clear

Fig 218   Same tack when overlapped (IYRU Rule 37.1).

The easiest way of remembering whether you are on starboard or port is that if your right hand is next to the mast then you are on starboard. This not only applies when sailing upwind but also works when on reaches and runs. However, if two boards are on starboard, Rule 2 comes into operation – this could occur on all points of sailing. (*See* Fig 218.)

Rule 2

Same tack when overlapped (IYRU Rule 37.1). 'A windward board shall keep clear of a leeward board.'

To decide whether you are overlapped, imagine a line drawn at right angles to the centre line of your board at the transom. If you are overlapped or about to be then it is the windward boat that must keep clear. This can happen when sailing to windward and you are not pointing as high as the board beneath you. It may also happen if both boards are on the same reach. Beware when sailing on the funboard 'M' type course, as when beating you will come across sailors on the reach. If you are both on the same tack, try to shout 'windward board' to the reaching windsurfer. They may not have seen you and the call will let them know that you are there. (*See* Fig 218.)

Rule 3

Same tack when not overlapped (IYRU Rule 37.2). 'A board clear astern shall keep clear of a board clear ahead.'

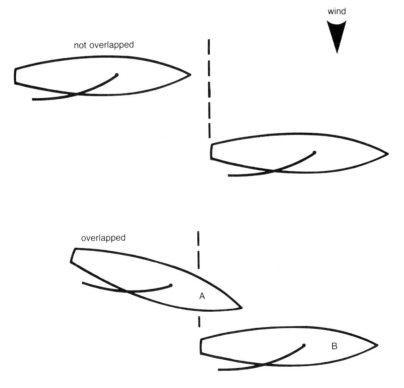

windward board (A), must keep clear

Fig 219   Same tack when not overlapped (IYRU Rule 37.2).

167

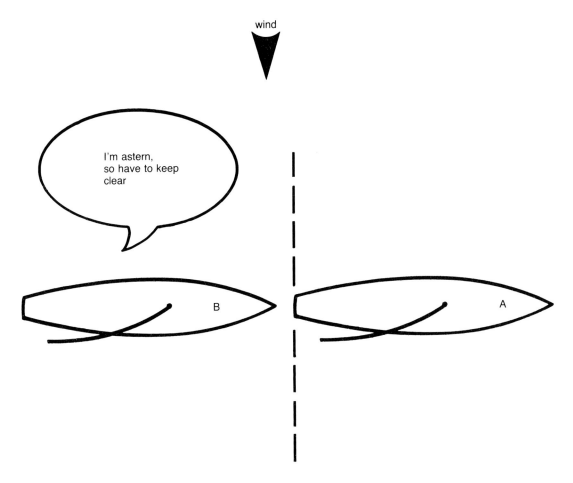

board B is astern since it is not overlapped

Fig 220   IYRU Rule 37.2 - the astern board keeps clear.

This is sometimes referred to as the 'over-taking' rule – if you are not overlapped then this rule applies. When in this position, if you are the overtaking board then you must keep clear. As you overtake to windward Rule 2 applies again – as you are now the windward board you again have to keep clear. A simple combination of rules 2 and 3 is that the overtaking board has to keep clear. (*See* Figs 219 and 220.)

Rule 4

Changing tacks – tacking and gybing (IYRU Rule 41). 'A board that is either tacking or gybing shall keep clear of a board sailing normally.'

The principle behind this rule is do not tack or gybe into someone else. It does not matter if you tack or gybe on to starboard and the other board is on port, this does not exonerate you.

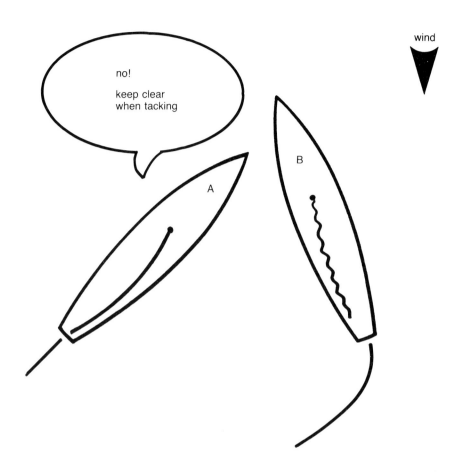

Fig 221 Tacking and gybing (IYRU Rule 41).

If the other board is forced to take avoiding action then you should not have tacked or gybed. Consider this before you change tacks. (*See* Fig 221.)

Rule 5

Rounding marks (IYRU Rule 42).

This is probably the most complex of the five rules, and also the most important as all wind-surfers will pass around marks, and by doing so be close together. It will not apply to the windward marks if you are on opposite tacks, but it will apply at all other marks where it takes precedent over Rules 1–4.

This rule controls the water within two board lengths of the mark, for example on course boards a circle of approximately 8m diameter from the mark. If you are astern and not over-lapped at two board lengths from the mark then you should anticipate the board in front slowing down to harden up or gybe around the mark.

If you are overlapped, as defined by Figure 218 then IYRU Rule 42.1 states 'An outside board shall give each inside overlapping board room to round or pass the mark'. Therefore, if you have positioned yourself on the inside at a

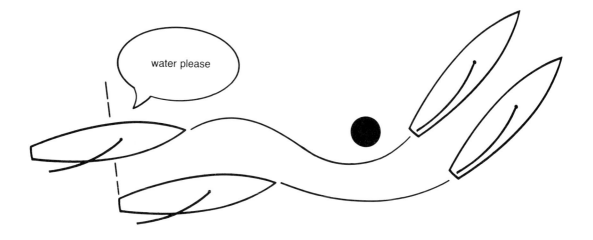

Fig 222   Rounding marks (IYRU Rule 42).

port and starboard are overidden by this rule

mark and have an overlap by the time the leading board reaches the two board circle then you will be given enough room to get around the mark.

The whole of Rule 42 is much more complicated but the above will get you racing. Remember that this rule overrides Rules 1–4 once you are inside two board lengths (*see* Fig 223).

The next point to look at is what to do if you commit an infringement. A board that acknowledges infringing a right of way rule or touches a mark may exonerate itself by sailing well clear of all other boards as soon as possible after the incident and remaining clear while it makes two full 360 degree turns in the same direction.

So if you do commit an infringement you can continue in the race as soon as you have performed a 720 degree turn, making sure that you keep well clear of all other boards while you are doing this. You have no rights while you are performing your turns.

Fig 223   IYRU Rule 42.1 - outside board should give inside over-lapping board room to pass a mark.

MORE ADVANCED RULES FOR COURSE RACING

Luffing

Sometimes in windsurfing races you will find that rather than sailing against a whole fleet of boards, you are simply one on one with another board. At times like these additional knowledge of the rules can be very useful. One such rule is luffing, which allows you to sail your opponent away from the direction he wants to go in – to clarify this, you need to know three definitions:

LUFFING – altering course towards the wind.
PROPER COURSE – any course that a board may sail after the starting signal, in the absence of other boards, that allows that board to finish as quickly as possible.
LUFFING RIGHTS – you have 'luffing rights' when you have the right to luff as quickly as you like right up to head to wind. A board that is clear ahead or a leeward board may luff as he/she pleases, except that he/she shall not sail above his/her proper course while an overlap

exists, if when the overlap began or at any time during its existence, the sailor of the windward board has been abreast or in front of the mast foot of the leeward board while standing in the normal position.

Now you can see why these are called 'advanced rules' for course racing! The diagrams in Figs 224 and 225 will hopefully clarify any confusion. Imagine that you are a windward overtaking board and as you overtake the board below you starts to luff; that board has 'luffing rights' as it has been clear ahead. This board may luff you as high as head to wind (on a beam reach this is 90 degree off your course); he may also turn into the wind as quickly as he likes. It is your responsibility to keep clear, but as you overtake the board, assuming that you are in your normal position, once you are opposite the leeward board's mast foot then you can call 'mast abeam'. This call will return the leeward board to its proper course immediately and curtail the luff. This is a very useful tactical ploy, particularly when you are down to two boards both fighting for the best position.

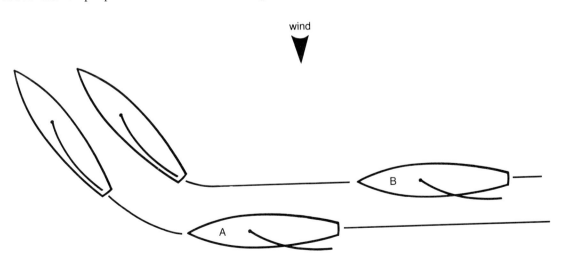

leeward board, A, luffs

Fig 224 The clear ahead leeward board has luffing rights.

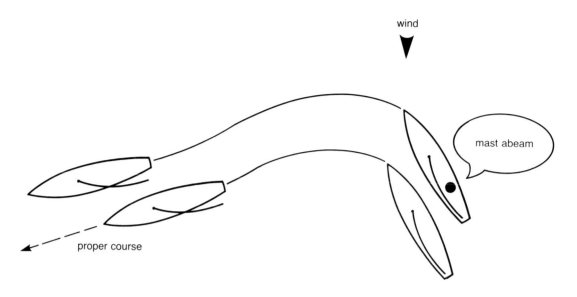

Fig 225 A call of 'mast abeam' returns the luffing board to its proper course.

Pumping

Pumping is another area of particular relevance to windsurfers, as a few pumps of the sail will quickly accelerate the board. However, you have to look at the rules first to find out if this means of propulsion is allowed in your race. In funboard racing you are allowed to pump as much as you like, while in Lechner, Division I, and some forms of one design racing you are restricted to a certain number of pumps per wave or gust of wind. This rule has caused a great deal of controversy in some clubs between dinghy-style windsurfers and funboard sailors. The dinghy-style windsurfers prefer close tactical racing to the physical element, hence they adopt the 'one pump per wave' rule as laid down in the IYRU rules. This pump can only be used to promote surfing or planing on that wave, so if you cannot surf, or are already planing, you cannot pump. Funboard sailors prefer the physical element and see pumping as a speed-related skill. The answer is to check the rules at your club, or at the event you are racing

in. It is then important that you respect these rules and sail to them, and try to change people's points of view later on in the bar by discussion, rather than out on the water!

FUNBOARD RULES

As previously discussed, funboard rules are slightly different to IYRU rules. Funboard rules are also controlled by the IYRU and appear as an appendix to the IYRU racing rules. Check which rules apply to you – look carefully at 'pumping' (IYRU Rule 54) and 'touching a mark' (IYRU Rule 52). In funboard racing you can pump and hit all marks with the exception of the start marks. Below you will find rules for slalom, wave and speed sailing competitions – it is important only to use these rules as a guide and to check your race instructions for the event carefully before going out on the water.

Right-of-Way Rules for Slalom

Boards on Opposite Tacks

(a) A competitor who is coming in shall keep clear of a competitor who is going out.
(b) When neither is coming in or going out, a competitor on port tack shall keep clear from a competitor on starboard tack.

Boards on the Same Tack/Gybing Around a Mark

(a) A competitor clear astern shall keep clear of a competitor clear ahead.
(b) An overtaking boat shall keep clear.

Changing Tacks, Tacking and Gybing

A competitor who is tacking or gybing, shall keep clear of a competitor on a tack, except when gybing around a mark.

Limitations on Altering Course

When one competitor is required to keep clear of another, the competitor with right of way shall not alter course so as to prevent the other from keeping clear, or so as to obstruct him/her while he/she is keeping clear.

Capsized Boards

(a) A competitor underway shall keep clear of one who is capsized.
(b) A competitor shall not be penalised for failure to keep clear of another who capsized immediately in front of him/her.
(c) A competitor who is capsized shall not take any action which hinders another competitor.

Right-of-Way Rules for Wave Performance

Boards on Opposite Tacks

A competitor who is coming in shall keep clear of a competitor who is going out.

Boards on the Same Wave, Coming In

When two or more competitors are on a wave coming in, a competitor who does not have possession shall keep clear.

Boards on the Same Tack and not on a Wave

(a) A competitor clear astern and not on a wave shall keep clear of a competitor clear ahead.
(b) An overtaking competitor who is not on a wave shall keep clear.

Boards in Transition

(a) A competitor who is in transition shall keep clear of a competitor on a tack.
(b) When two competitors are in transition at the same time, the one on the other's port side shall keep clear.

Capsized Boards

(a) A competitor under way shall keep clear of one who is capsized.
(b) A competitor shall not be penalised for failure to keep clear of another who capsized immediately in front of him.
(c) A competitor who is capsized shall not take any action which hinders another competitor.

Some Special Rules for Speed Sailing Competitions

1. Sail numbers – the sail number will be displayed on both sides of the sail, starboard

side highest, in the top half of the sail, a minimum of 38cm high x 19cm wide (excluding number 1). The numbers will be on a white background and a minimum of 5cm apart. The background should provide a minimum of 5cm border.

2. Signals

Red flags – officials are standing by but timing is not taking place.

Green flags – course open, timing taking place.

Red and White answering pennant:

Flown with or without red or green flags – A change in signals will take place within five minutes.

All flags dropped at the end of the day – course closed for the day.

3. All flag signals will be displayed at the start and finish of the course where possible. (On 250m courses they may only be displayed at the start.)

4. Starting area: there will be a defined starting area divided into two and marked with buoys.

Area A – an area commencing 200m from the start in which no beach or water starting is allowed, except to sail off the course by the quickest route possible to avoid hindering competitors who are starting properly. No overtaking is allowed. Area A is entered through a narrow gate 2–3m wide.

Area B – an area commencing approximately 75m from the start in which all the rules of A apply and only one board at a time is allowed.

5. On the course: while on the course no beach or waterstarting is allowed except as stated in A.

6. Finishing area: a finishing area will be defined by a mark 60m after the finish mark, in which no competitor may stop or sail other than from the course (except in an emergency).

7. Tandem precedence: all sailors will give way to, and not hinder, Tandem or Tridem, at all times.

8. Returning to the start: competitors returning to the start must keep to the leeward side of the course unless special rules governing return in various venues or conditions apply.

14 Advanced Racing Strategy

When talking about getting better at racing the first thing you think about is improving speed, but there is another aspect which can offer greater gains and is often overlooked and that is being *clever*! A clever-thinking sailor will always beat a windsurfer of similar speed. In this chapter we will look at aspects of windsurfing, not related to speed or board/body preparation, that will give you an edge. We will consider the 'M' type course, now used for course racing in Division I, Division II and most popular windsurfing formats. Many of the same rules can also be applied to slalom racing.

Windsurfing is a very open and variable sport. Just look at the water, smooth one day, choppy the next, or possibly with such a shore-break that just getting out beyond it becomes a victory in itself. Consider also the wind, the means of propulsion: it is very inconsistent, both in velocity and direction, and it is this that will give the thinking windsurfer the upper hand.

When referring to the thinking windsurfer, we mean a windsurfer who will learn by his and others' experiences, someone who will question elements and strive to have further knowledge about his sport. This person may not be the fastest on the water, but more times than not he will arrive at the finish line first simply by sailing a more sensible course, taking advantage of the wind, tide and other windsurfers' positions.

GUSTS

Having decided that you should be combining speed, preparation and a bit of thinking in your windsurfing, what should you know about the wind in which you windsurf? The increase/decrease in velocity of the wind should already form part of your windsurfing skills. Looking for gusts as they track down towards you should be part of your upwind technique. It is certainly easier to handle an overpowered rig when you know about and can prepare for a gust prior to it arriving, again your vision will be the key factor in isolating wind velocity increase/decrease. As a rule, the lighter the wind the further you will have to look upwind to find valuable information; in sub-planing conditions you will need to look at least half a beat upwind. As the wind decreases to drifting-type conditions, you need to survey the whole beat before committing yourself to going to the left or right.

BENDS AND SHIFTS

Changes in wind angles (eg windshifts) are harder to detect. They fall into the two broad categories of oscillating winds and persistent shifts. Persistent shifts are the easiest to understand as the wind slowly moves in one direction. This can be caused by a headland, valley or shoreline, if you are sailing inland or close to the shore. The movement of the wind in one direction on the sea may also be caused by the arrival of a new wind, ie a sea breeze – another term for this type of occurrence is a wind bend.

The action to take on a beat if this does occur is to make sure that your board is the inside board – nearest the bend. Just imagine the wind bend as a running track, with you needing to be in Lane 1 rather than Lane 8. When this happens, the earlier you cut your losses and get to the inside of the bend the better and it does not matter if you have to go behind boards to achieve this.

The actions are clear when sailing in a wind bend; the only problem is that you have to be sure that the bend is permanent and that it will not go back to its original direction – performing the role of an oscillating shift, as the actions for oscillating winds and persistant shifts are opposite to each other.

	OSCILLATING WIND	WIND BEND
LIFTED	Stay on the same tack as you gain on others who are on the opposite tack.	If this is a bend look for other boards and position yourself on the inside of the bend.
HEAD-ED	Tack as soon as possible.	If heading for the inside of the bunch of boards hold course. If inside tack.

As to whether you are being lifted or headed, this can be judged by boards around you. If you look as if you are powering over a board to leeward, you are either being lifted or going more quickly. If you are doing this to a number of boards, then you are probably being lifted. Conversely, if you are not pointing as high as someone else, you may be headed and the more sudden the change in headings, the more likely that you have been affected by an oscillating shift.

In an oscillating wind you can be in one of three sectors, on the average direction or either

side. Obviously, if sailing on a tack this means that you are being lifted, headed or sailing on the mean wind. To sail the fastest route, it is best if you can sail on the lifting tack all the time. If you get headed, then in order to sail on the lifting tack, you will need to tack, consequently by tacking on the shifts you can always be on the favoured tack as you progress up the beat. Just be aware of the position of the windward mark; sometimes by tacking on each shift you may not end up at the windward mark. Experience will also dictate how big the shift needs to be to make it worthwhile tacking. Once you are planing upwind, these shifts have to be relatively big as you will lose more time by tacking than you will gain on the shift. The rule is, the faster you are going the larger the shift has to be before you gain any advantage through tacking.

LAYLINES

The area that can be sailed within while on a beat to the windward mark is defined by laylines. A layline is the close hauled course taken, either on port or starboard, to arrive at the windward mark. If you sail beyond the layline, you are throwing distance away. Tacking short of the layline will result in having to do extra tacks, while throwing away valuable distance. Deciding when to tack is related to experience, depending on the type of board, wind speed and tacking angle, but the further you are away from the mark, the harder it will be to judge. Devise a system so that if you turn your head, you can see the mark, then with experience you will be able to judge how far into your field of vision the buoy needs to be before you can tack. If you misjudge your approach to the mark, the extra time lost through tacking can be very considerable in terms of distance lost to those sailors who have chosen the correct layline.

A problem with laylines is that once on them you have no options should the wind shift.

As mentioned earlier, for each tack, you sail on the mean, or are lifted or headed. Once on the layline this still applies, so if you are on the mean nothing is lost, but if you are lifted you will have sailed extra distance and will have to bear off. If you are headed, then you cannot tack as you would then sail away from the mark. If you are not on the layline then you still have the option of being on either tack. The other problem of being on a layline is that you can be a long distance from other boards, for example on a one mile beat, two boards on opposite extremes of the course may be up to a mile apart. This distance would be significant if there were to be a wind shift. For a 10° wind shift one board will gain 25 per cent of the distance between them and 25 per cent of a mile is a long way! In order to gamble less distance you must keep a watchful eye on the rest of the fleet and ensure that you are close to them. Only go off on your own if you are 100 per cent certain that you are right and that the rest of the fleet are going the wrong way up the beat. This will generally only happen if a new wind (a sea breeze for example) is starting to affect you and you are the first person to see it arriving.

Vision and observance are the key ingredients in making gains, but, of course, when you start racing you will be more concerned with getting the maximum speed from your board. Once your board handling improves then you can concentrate more on the wind and waves. Remember that when you are not concentrating on speed you can concentrate more on what is happening around you.

STARTING

Starting is a skill in itself, and can be split into three areas of strategy, board handling and rules. The rule area is relatively small; you just need enough knowledge to keep out of trouble. Board handling can be improved with specific practice. The tricky part where most experience counts is in deciding which is the best place

to start on the start line. Bias is the key word; this describes the discrepancy between the wind and the start line. If the start line is at 90 degrees to the wind, then the line has no bias. If this is not the case, then the start line has bias, and presents an opportunity on which you can capitalise. If you start at the biased end of the line you will have less distance to travel to the windward mark. (*See* Fig 226).

To establish the bias sail along the start line, being careful to trim the sail as accurately as possible. The boom angle is the key factor. Once you are happy with the angle, turn around and sail back along the line, again checking the angle of boom. Decide on which tack you were sailing closer to the wind (boom closest to the centre line). You are now sailing to the end of the start line which is biased. This system works for all upwind starts. Do remember that if everyone decides that one or other end of the line is biased this will cause congestion, and so is best avoided if you do not think your slow, close quarter board handling is good enough to allow you a good start.

For downwind starts practise sailing at the mark. This will give you an idea of the angle that you will be sailing at. This is the key factor in deciding at which end to start. The broader the angle the slower you will go, so you need to have experience of whether a shorter, broader and slower course is quicker than a longer, tighter course. If the tighter course is also nearer, then obviously there is no decision – start at that end. Also consider the effect of wind shadow – sometimes this can be negated if you can time your run to perfection. Recognising gaps will be particularly positive in gaining good starts not only for upwind starts but also for reaching starts. The advantage of having a gap below you is that you have the option of cracking off to gain additional speed, which may allow you to sail over the board to leeward – again experience is the key factor in being successful here. Learn not only from your own experience, but also the experience of others, to shorten your learning cycle.

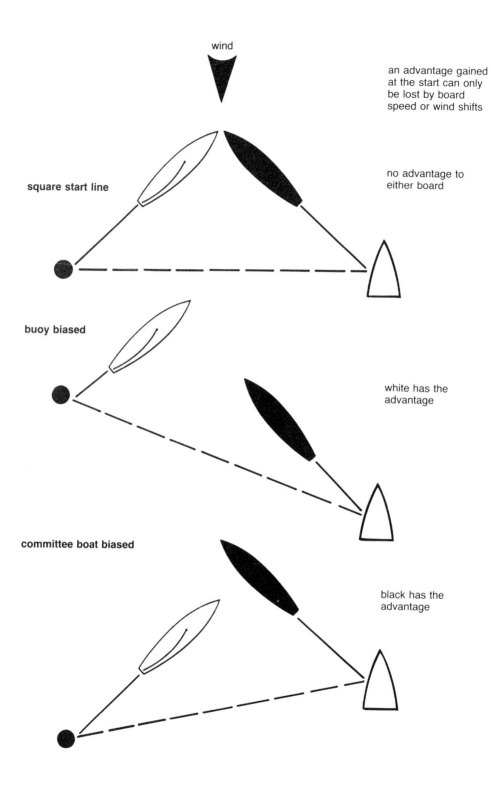

wind

an advantage gained
at the start can only
be lost by board
speed or wind shifts

no advantage to
either board

square start line

buoy biased

white has the
advantage

committee boat biased

black has the
advantage

Fig 226 Starting techniques for advanced racing strategy.

Fig 227   Leading board has right of way in slalom racing.

MARK ROUNDINGS

Marks will present unique opportunities for gaining places, particularly gybe marks in fun-board, one design and development class racing. The reason for this is Rule 42, which will allow an inside overlapped board 'ample room and opportunity' to round the mark, for example if you just have an overlap, 0.5m of your board ahead of the tail of the leading board, then, as long as this was achieved two board lengths from the mark, you can gybe closest to the mark. In reality this will give you a two board length advantage with you exiting the mark first with the previous leading board now in your chop and dirty air. Obviously on an 'M' course the preferred option of low or high on the reach will change as you go around

the gybe marks, normally it will be low until the last reach to the leeward mark where it will be high, in all cases allowing you to be the inside board. On close reaches in gusty winds beware of the lower option, as the gusts will allow those to windward to accelerate over the top (*see* Fig 227).

In slalom racing this does not apply as leading board has right of way, so the windward overtaking option is the favourite, unless the leg is broad in which case careful use of gusts will allow you to work below someone on a long reaching leg. Bear away in gusts and luff slightly in the lulls, all the time trying to keep good speed so that the apparent wind speed advantage is maintained.

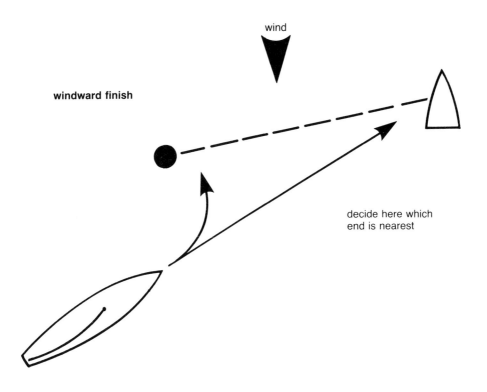

wind

windward finish

decide here which
end is nearest

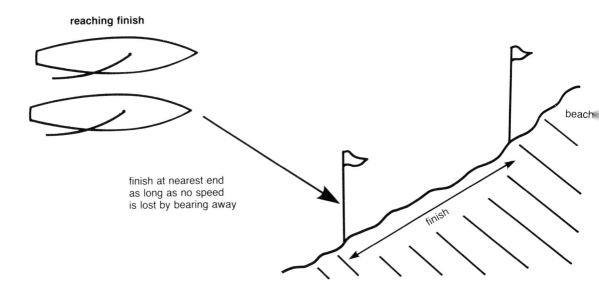

reaching finish

finish at nearest end
as long as no speed
is lost by bearing away

beach

finish

Fig 228   Finishing techniques for advanced racing strategy.

FINISHING

Finishing lines, just like start lines, will present the opportunity for gain, the reason again being line bias, as one end is favoured due to the angle of the wind. For long board racing as you approach the finish, start to look upwind for the line normally a boat and a buoy. As you hit a layline you will be able to judge which end is closest, buoy or boat. If a big difference is involved, go for the shortest distance; if the difference is small then you will have to decide if tacking is worthwile (you lose distance due to the time taken and you will be on port/starboard – look for other approaching boards). Having considered these options, you will be able to decide to which end to sail (*see* Fig 228).

Angles will again be important in downwind finishes on course racing and slalom. If the leeward end of the finishing line is a lower course but closer, then you have the options of lower and slower, or further and faster. Again experience is a key factor in knowing how much faster without losing too much speed. To make your decision consider the following:

1. Position in fleet.
2. Waves.
3. Wind speed (gusts, etc).

If you are leading, go for the high course; you can always bear away if the lower option looks better. Waves may allow you to bear off; use them to pick up speed and shoot through without losing speed due to wind shadow from the boards to windward. Gusty winds will always favour the higher option unless you are overpowered. You need experience to recognise the interaction of all the variables, and you will have lots of fun racing to gain this.

This chapter simply gives you insight into areas that you should look at for tactical gains. The experience factor is high, and more knowledge of tidal considerations can be gained from specific dinghy racing books. Try to learn from each race and ask others. This is all part of the social side of windsurfing racing. Combining these skills with the preparation and board handling skills examined in other chapters, should allow you to find a windsurfing discipline in which you gain tremendous enjoyment through competition.

15 Organising Your Own Club Competitions

As we have emphasised in this book, competition is primarily for fun and is the best way to get everyone involved in the sport. Competing is a great way to meet people and break the ice between new windsurfers joining your club or group. Competition also ensures safer windsurfing for everyone, as it tends to keep people together so that you are always in sight of someone who can come to your aid if necessary. Besides, competition is the best way to improve everyone's standards so it should be encouraged as much as possible. So that you can organise your own competitions we have listed some ideas and described how to carry them out. With a little imagination and enthusiasm windsurfing has endless options and is the best way we know of spending a sunny summer afternoon with friends!

KNOCK-OUT FREESTYLE

This type of freestyle differs from conventional freestyle in that, instead of each competitor taking his or her turn to perform their routine, everyone performs their tricks at the same time. This overcomes time problems and competitors being too self-conscious to compete.

What You Need

1. A list of tricks, starting from the very easy and progressively getting harder.
2. A loudhailer (or club member with a loud voice!).

3. Judges – their numbers depend on the numbers of competitors.

What You Do

Give a short briefing to competitors, explaining the competition area and the rules. The course area should be large enough for everyone to be able to compete without collisions, but small enough for the judges to be able to see what is happening. Shout out the name of the first trick on your list and give everyone a suitable length of time to complete it. Anyone who falls in or is unable to complete the trick is immediately out of the competition. It is the rôle of the judges to spot these people. Once you are satisfied that everyone who failed on the first trick has left the course area, shout out the second trick – continue your list of tricks until there is only one person left in the course area, this is the winner. If you want to encourage participation, you can give competitors three lives, but this is harder to police.

Suggested List of Tricks

1. Sail with only one hand.
2. Sail on one foot.
3. Sit on board.
4. Sail clew first.
5. Sail backwards.
6. Sail clew first backwards.
7. Flare gybe.
8. One foot rail ride.
9. Back to sail.

10. Back leaning into sail.
11. Sail 360.
12. Spin tack.
13. Pirouette.
14. Spin gybe.
15. Two feet on the rail.
16. Duck tack.
17. Back to sail on the rail.
18. Somersault through the booms.

See Chapter 8 for more tricks.

BUOY BALL

Buoy ball is an entertaining game to play when there is little wind.

You Will Need

1. Flat water.
2. Four small buoys to designate two goal areas about 25m apart. The goals need to be about 1m wide.
3. A large beach ball (preferably one with ears to use as handles!).
4. Two teams of an equal number of people – preferably more than four in each team – the more people there are the more fun it is!
5. It is useful to have a referee in a rubber-sided boat on the water, but you can manage without.
6. Durable boards and rigs for each competitor.

How to Play

First, decide which team is going to start with the ball – if you cannot decide the referee sends everyone back behind their goal lines and leaves the ball in the centre of the pitch, and when he signals the start the teams sail out from behind their lines to try to get the ball. The idea is to score as many goals as possible and the team which scores the most goals wins. A player is allowed to either sail with or throw the ball, as

soon as the holder of the ball is tackled or touched by an opponent he or she must throw the ball. If this is not done immediately, the ball is given to the opposition. Play for a short time – perhaps ten minutes, then change ends to make sure the competition is fair. If there is no wind at all competitors can leave their rigs on shore and paddle their boards.

SLALOM COMPETITIONS

Slalom competitions are always popular with both competitors and spectators and can be held in any wind strength. All you need are two or more buoys and a little wind. Try to arrange the buoys so that you can sail a course between them across the wind. If you have more than two buoys arrange them so that you are continually sailing a downwind course – *see* Chapter 4. You can either separate competitors into heats, or if you have a low number of entries you can start everybody together. Before the start, gather everybody together and tell them the course including how many laps you want them to do and where the start and finish lines are. If you are just using two buoys you can have the start and finish line further down the beach so that the start line can be used for running more heats.

Two on a Board Slalom

This is a progression of normal slalom. The same rules and instructions apply as for conventional slalom.

RELAY AND BLINDFOLD RACES

These are self-explanatory and can be sailed on any course format that you have.

PURSUIT WINDSURFING

This type of windsurfing competition enables sailors of all abilities using different types of boards to race together in a manner which will be rewarding and exciting for everyone. A personal handicap system (similar to the system used in golf) is the basis of pursuit windsurfing.

Each competitor is allocated a handicap number on their ability or finishing position in an earlier race. Each person starts at a different time depending on their handicap number. the starts are indicated by a hooter.

0 = 1st starter
1 = 1 minute time handicap
2 = 2 minute time handicap
3 = 3 minute time handicap
4 = 4 minute time handicap
5 = 5 minute time handicap, and so on.

The starter makes sound or visual signals at one minute intervals. Each minute signal represents the start time for that handicap number, where 1 = 1, 2 = 2, etc. Boards start from the beach and the timer is the person who will start last – the person who won the previous race. This person has the job of blowing the horn for everyone to start before setting off in hot pursuit himself.

The course is a conventional 'M' or triangle course.

Finishing

When 30 minutes have expired from the time the first board left the beach a horn is sounded and the next mark to be rounded by the leader is the finishing mark. As competitors round the mark they should make a mental note of their position relative to who is behind and in front of them. When they return to shore the positions are noted and handicaps updated for the next race.

If you have a large fleet with over twenty racing you will need a finishing boat to keep track of the names of people finishing and assist in any possible rescue.

Scoring System

Below is an example of a results sheet used for the pursuit windsurfing handicap system.

First and second place in each race add one minute to their original handicap rating. Third and fourth keep the same rating, fifth and below subtract one minute from their rating.

CONVENTIONAL COURSE RACING

Conventional course racing can be run quite adequately without the use of boats and committees if you have a safe venue such as a harbour or lake.

NAME	HANDICAP	RACE 1	HANDICAP	RACE 2	HANDICAP
NAISH	10	1	+1 = 11	3	= 11
BRINGDAL	2	2	+1 = 3	2	+1 = 4
ANDREWS	5	3	= 5	4	= 5
BLOGGS	4	4	= 4	5	−1 = 3
WAY	6	5	−1 = 5	1	+1 = 6

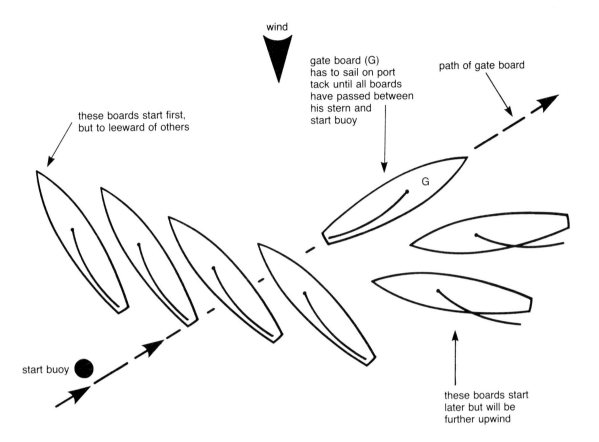

wind

gate board (G)
has to sail on port
tack until all boards
have passed between
his stern and
start buoy

path of gate board

these boards start first,
but to leeward of others

G

start buoy

these boards start
later but will be
further upwind

Fig 229   In a gate start everyone gets an equal start.

The Course

This can be an 'M' course or three buoy triangle course. You can often pick out a course from buoys or boats already in the water. The number of laps and the finishing mark is decided at the briefing.

The Start

The fairest way to start a fleet without a conventional start system is with a gate start (*see* Fig 227). The person who finished fifth in the previous race is normally gate board. Competitors are told where the start area is and which buoy the gate board starts from.

When everybody is in the start area, the gate board sails as close to the wind as possible on port tack from the buoy towards the fleet. The fleet has to pass behind and to leeward of the gate board – they have to pass between his stern and the buoy that he started from (*see* Fig 229). Competitors are not allowed to hit the gate board.

The Finish

The first board to the finish is the winner. He/she then has to record the positions of all the rest. One good way to do this is to attach a pencil and waterproof board to the finishing mark.

Scoring

Use the funboard course racing scoring system which is:

1st = 0.7 points.   3rd = 3 points.
2nd = 2 points.   4th = 4 points, etc.

After four races the competitors may discard their worst result. Club racers normally prefer plenty of short races, rather than fewer longer ones.

Useful Addresses

UNITED KINGDOM WINDSURFING

The Royal Yachting Association
RYA House
Romsey Road
Eastleigh
Southampton   SO5 4YA
Tel: 0703 629962   Telex: 47393 BOATIN–G
Fax: 0703 629924

The United Kingdom Boardsailing Association
(UKBSA)
Masons Road
Stratford-upon-Avon
Warwickshire   CV37 9NZ
Tel: 0789 299574

The British Windsurfing Association (BWA)
and The British Speedsailing Association (BSA)
163 West Lane
Hayling Island
Hampshire
Tel: 0705 463595

The International Mistral Class Organisation of
Great Britain (IMCOGB)
2 Southwold
Bracknell
Berkshire   RG12 4XY
Tel: 0344 422844

The International Windsurfer Class Association
of Great Britain (IWCAGB)
2 Denmark Road
Reading
Berkshire   RG1 5PA

Seavets (Senior and Veterans Boardsailing
Association)
9 Ferndale Gardens
Hook
Basingstoke
Hampshire   RH27 9DR
Tel: 0256 722322

Scottish Windsurfing Association (SWA)
18 Ainslee Place
Edingburgh   EH3 6AU
Tel: 031 226401

Women's Windsurfing UK (WWUK)
Tel: 01 558 3171

British Student Windsurfing (BSW)
Tel: 0532 570788

INTERNATIONAL WINDSURFING

The Canadian Yachting Association (CYA)
333 River Road
Vanier
Ottawa
Ontario   K1L 8B9
Canada

The United States Boardsailing Association
(USBA)
PO Box 206
Oyster Bay
NY 117711
USA

Useful Addresses

The New Zealand Yachting Federation
PO Box 4173
Auckland
New Zealand

The Australian Yachting Federation
33 Peel Street
Milson's Point
NSW 2061
Australia

The World Boardsailing Association (WBA)
Feldafinder Platz 2
71   München   8000
West Germany

The World Speedsailing Association
PO Box 351
Hove
Sussex   BN3 2PW
UK

The International Mistral Class Association
(IMCA)
Grindel Strasse 11
8303 Bassendorf
Switzerland

The International Yacht Racing Union (IYRU)
60 Knightsbridge
London   SW1X 7JX
UK

Glossary

Apparent wind   Wind that you feel when you are moving and that differs from true wind that exists when standing still.

Battens   Glass fibre strips that slot into the sail to create a more rigid profile.

Beach start   A way of starting in shallow water by stepping straight on to the board without using the uphaul.

Bearing away   Steering away from the wind.

Beating   Sailing the closest course possible to the wind.

Bottom turn   A high speed turn at the bottom of a wave.

Camber inducer   A piece of plastic that rotates around the mast into which the batten slots thus giving the sail a more aerodynamic shape.

Carve gybe   A gybe done in planing conditions without a centreboard. The board is turned by foot pressure, not the sail.

Centreboard   Used on high volume boards to help them sail upwind, it is retracted into the board when going downwind in strong winds. It can also be called a daggerboard.

Chop   Small waves, often close together.

Cleat   A small fitting used to secure control lines.

Clew   The back corner of the sail that is attached to the end of the boom.

Close hauled   The course you sail when beating.

Concaves   A slight curving on the underside of boards which produces greater speed.

Course racing   A discipline which involves sailing around a large course marked by buoys. The course normally involves mainly upwind work.

Cut back   A wave sailing manoeuvre consisting of a sharp turn made at the top of a wave.

Custom board   A board made specifically to order.

Dirty wind   Windflow which has been disturbed by obstacles such as another board or cliffs.

Downhaul   The line that controls the tension of the luff.

Duck gybe   A gybe similar to the carve gybe but where the boom passes over the head of the sailor.

Duck tack   A tack involving ducking under the sail – a freestyle manoeuvre.

Foot   The bottom of the sail.

Freestyle   A competitive discipline which involves the sailor performing tricks.

Funboard   A term used to describe a board that performs well in over eleven knots of wind.

Gate start   A method of starting a fleet of boards.

Gybing   Turning the board around away from the wind, allowing the sail to pass over the front of the board.

Harness   A device which takes the strain off a sailor's arms and which can be worn around the chest, waist or seat. It has a hook attached to it which connects to lines from the booms.

Inhaul   The line that attaches the boom to the mast.

Leeward   The side of the board furthest from the wind. (Opposite to windward.)

Luff   The front of the sail.

Luffing   Making another sailor head up into the wind.

One design   Used to describe boards that are uniform and which cannot be altered.

Planing   Sailing at sufficient speed to allow the board to skim the surface of the water rather than go through it.

Port   Left. If your left hand is closest to the mast – port tack.

Rail   The edge of the board.

Railriding   Sailing on the side of the board – a freestyle manoeuvre.

Reaching   Sailing with the wind blowing at or near right angles to the board.

Sail numbers   The numbers which are used to identify competitors in races.

Sheeting in   To pull in on the boom with your back hand.

Slalom   A competitive form of windsurfing involving reaching and gybing around a series of marks.

Skeg   The piece of protruding plastic on the underside tail of the board that helps keep it sailing in a straight line.

Spinout   A problem that can occur when reaching at high speed – the skeg loses grip and the board starts to slide sideways.

Starboard   Right. If your right hand is closest to the mast – starboard tack.

Tacking   Turning the board through the eye of the wind and stepping around the front of the mast.

Trimming   Adjusting the board and sail to the prevailing conditions.

True wind   The wind you experience when stationary.

Uphauling   Pulling the sail out of the water using the uphaul rope.

Volume   The amount of material in the board which determines its buoyancy.

Waterstart   Getting on to the board without uphauling in deep water.

Wetsuit   A neoprene suit that keeps you warm in the water.

Windshift   A change in the direction of the wind.

Windward   The side of the board closest to the wind. (The opposite to leeward.)

Index

Index